ADVANCE PRAISE F

"For everyone wanting to understand more about our journey as Black Women On the Move, read this! An easy read, filled with stories, that gathers us, wraps its arms around us, and says to us, 'You. Are. Worthy.' I can already hear the *Mm hmms* that will accompany the flipping of pages."
—Guylaine Saint Juste, President and CEO, NABA Inc.

"*Access Denied* is the most compelling, insightful, and in some instances, painstaking read about workplace disparities and discrimination. Although I was not unaware or surprised about these experiences, it was, nonetheless, a gut-punch reminder about ever-present challenges faced by people of color, especially African Americans, navigating the complexities of the workplace. A must-READ, not just for us, but for all!!!!"
—Dr. Shiela Harmon Martin
Professor of Political Science
Former Chair, Division of Social & Behavioral Sciences
University of the District of Columbia

"In a time when social justice issues are finally coming to the forefront, *Access Denied* is a timely resource to help employees, managers, and organizations create needed strategies for talent development. I have collaborated with and followed Brenda Harrington's work for over eight years, and I am looking forward to learning more from her to help my own managerial practices become more equitable."
—Kimberly A. Carlson, PhD, Co-Founder/CEO Tractus Strategic Partners
Associate Professor of Practice in Management, Virginia Tech

"Rarely does an author strike such a profound balance between reality and optimism. Harrington has done so in this book, calling out racism and calling on individuals to stand up, speak out, and go boldly after their goals and desires. Spotlighting disturbing realities, asking deeply pointed questions, and offering unflinching strategies, this book needs to be read by those in both minority and majority groups."

—Lisa Hope Tilstra, MHS, PCC
Creator of the podcast, Make Life Less Difficult
https://makelifelessdifficult.com/

"*Access Denied* is a must-read for white leaders as it raises awareness of prejudice and discrimination in the workplace. I am humbled by Brenda's honesty and admire her willingness to share her very personal stories to support people of color who feel alone."

—Lisa T. Rees, Principal, LTR Leadership

"I think everyone working in Corporate America should read this book. It's not only a guide for Black people to navigate through the unfairness and inequality that is our everyday, but it will provide our white counterparts with a glimpse into what is causing these valid feelings. Most of us do not complain; instead, we work harder and longer to get to the 'middle.' I believe this book will help us work smarter, build mental fortitude, and find the words to speak up for ourselves when necessary. Thank you, Brenda, for listening to the stories and providing the tools we need to give us the courage to stay and be acknowledged for all the right reasons."

—Human Resources Executive, Hospitality Industry

"In the wake of George Floyd's horrific murder, legions of unaware and unconscious people finally got a glimpse of the inequities and injustices marginalized groups have endured for centuries. This 'in your face' event resulted in corporate investments to address cultural disparities, which is well intended and appreciated. However, deeply embedded and systemic issues require much more than what is often a surface-level solution. In *Access Denied*, Brenda has highlighted challenges marginalized people face in the workplace and uncovered what many in this community are experiencing. Stories of lived experiences are shared, practical advice is provided, and exercises are offered so that those impacted have opportunities to work through simulations to reinforce learning. *Access Denied* offers insight for anyone in the majority group who leads marginalized individuals; it's a reality check and reminder of how bias influences behavior and ultimate outcomes. This is a must-read for those who have felt the impact of workplace discrimination. Ms. Harrington has put forth tools to work through these challenges in a positive and productive way."

—Karen Mack, MSOD, ACC
Organization Development Practitioner and Leadership Coach

"In *Access Denied*, while a valued focus for a particular audience, Brenda is indeed writing of the human story. Her experience and the stories she chronicles are reflected in and exposed through day-to-day living that other people also experience in life. We can all learn to be better people by allowing these stories to challenge our assumptions and support us as we live and work with our common humanity each day."

—Leigh Shields
Executive Coach

"I have had numerous experiences with workplace disparities and discrimination throughout my career. Like most people of color, I continuously strive to find my place in the workplace. *Access Denied* is very encouraging. It's the read I needed in my pocket throughout my career. Moving forward with it will be a game changer. We must provide tools to assist our people and provide them better ways to make headway in the corporate system. *Access Denied* provides individuals with real life experiences and the tools needed to see through the games being played. As I approach the end of my career and strive to leave our loved ones with a sense of encouragement, guidance, and wealth, I feel this book provides them with another tool. It should be a required read for all people of color at any age, especially young individuals entering the workforce at all educational levels."

—Kenneth Robinson
Computer Scientist and Adjunct Professor

**Addressing Workplace
Disparities and Discrimination**

BRENDA HARRINGTON

South Columbus Avenue Press

conversations@access-denied.net
www.access-denied.net

Limits of Liability and Disclaimer of Warranty:
The authors and/or publisher shall not be liable for your misuse of this material. The contents are strictly for informational and educational purposes only.

ISBN:
Paperback: 979-8-9856426-0-5
Hardback: 979-8-9856426-1-2
Ebook: 979-8-9856426-2-9

Library of Congress Control Number: 2022902101

Publisher's Cataloging-in-Publication data

Names: Harrington, Brenda, author.
Title: Access denied : addressing workplace disparities and discrimination / Brenda Harrington.
Description: Includes bibliographical references. | South Columbus Avenue Press: Ashburn, VA, 2022.
Identifiers: LCCN: 2022902101 | ISBN: 979-8-9856426-1-2 (hardcover) | 979-8-9856426-0-5 (paperback) | 979-8-9856426-2-9 (ebook)
Subjects: LCSH Discrimination in employment. | Discrimination in employment--United States--Prevention. | Racism in the workplace. | Diversity in the workplace--UnitedStates.|Racerelations--UnitedStates.|Laborlawsandlegislation--United States. | Personnel management. | Corporate culture. | BISAC BUSINESS & ECONOMICS / Workplace Harassment & Discrimination | BUSINESS & ECONOMICS / Workplace Culture | LAW / Discrimination | LAW / Labor & Employment.
Classification: LCC HF5549.5.H37 2022 | DDC 658.30089--dc23

Published by South Columbus Avenue Press
Printed and bound in the United States of America

AN INVITATION

A primary purpose of this book is to start a conversation among members of the BIPOC community about how each of us can have greater influence on our own destiny. This is only the beginning. Through the development of additional media, and a series of peer groups that enable you to see yourself and others like you, we want this to be a safe place to explore and work through common challenges.

We invite you to join us as we continue the conversation! Please visit www.access-denied.net/letstalk to share your interest and preferences for keeping in touch.

DEDICATION

This book is dedicated to my husband and best friend, Jim Harrington. For more than 35 years, Jim has encouraged me to live into my aspirations and be all of who I am. He has been and continues to be an unwavering source of support and strength, whether skies are blue or gray. Thank you for living the true meaning of love.

ACKNOWLEDGMENTS

My heartfelt thanks goes to my one and only sister, Yvonne Curtis, for our early conversations about the book, for sharing her story, and inspiring an introduction that provided just the right foundation!

Special appreciation goes to the eight contributors who shared nine personal, and in some cases painful stories with me in the interest of forming this healing collective. Thank you for trusting me with such intimate elements of your experiences, and for your commitment to helping others who face similar circumstances take a different approach to working toward desired outcomes.

To my dear friend and human resources aficionado, Sharon Batiste McEwen. Thank you for helping me, and helping me help others navigate countless experiences involving indifference in the workplace.

A special thank you to you, Renee Harrington, for your guidance and counsel over the years, generously sharing the knowledge and experience you gained as an EEO professional.

Finally, to Douglas Harrington. Thank you for joining me on this journey as a thought and discussion partner, and for your immeasurable contribution to this work.

CONTENTS

Foreword by Christy Pichichero, PhD............................ 1

Introduction... 7

Section I: The Impact of Early Experiences 13

   1) Identity and Our Perception of Ourselves 15

   2) The Imprint of Early Experiences 25
      Story I: You Should Try Something Else.................. 28

Section II: Entering the World of Work 35

   3) Welcome to Corporate Life 37
      Story II: Notes to Myself.. 40

   4) Cracking the Code 49
      Story III: What Did I Do? 58
      Story IV: You Will Never Go Anywhere in This
      Organization 61

   5) Names and Faces.. 65
      Story V: The Trusted Advisor................................. 67
      Story VI: Stealing My Joy....................................... 72

   6) Expectations and the Psychological Contract.............. 83
      Story VII: Welcome Home 88

   7) Maintaining Your Identity... 95
      Story VIII: A Message from One of America's
      Founding Fathers.. 99

8) In Search of Safe Places 103

    Story IX: Withdraw Your Application,

       Your Colleague Is a Better Choice..................... 104

    Story X: The Dean Thinks You Should Leave;

       He Feels You Are Burned Out........................... 105

    Story XI: You Are Not Entitled to Be Here 107

    Story XII: I Think You're the Best Person

       to Facilitate a Discussion on Diversity 109

9) Speaking Up, Calling Things Out 111

Conclusion.. 125

Resources 129

A Note from the Author.. 130

About the Author.. 132

About the Illustrator.. 134

FOREWORD BY CHRISTY PICHICHERO, PHD

> *I recall feeling like I was in trouble, but I hadn't done anything wrong.*

> You will never go anywhere in this organization. You should try something else.

> *It appeared there was much more at play than an objective evaluation of my work based on documented results.*

> I didn't think you would fit in. Why can't you be more like her?

> *Have you lost your mind, or do you just think I've lost mine?*

> *I stood alone.*

Over the course of your education and career, have you ever felt a nebulous sense of disapproval coming from your superiors? Have you been underestimated, undermined, or unfairly evaluated? Have you experienced a sense of self-doubt and isolation? Have you been told or have you overheard statements like

1

these regarding your potential, your upward movement, or your "fit" in the culture of an organization? The above phrases, and many others examined by Brenda Harrington in this invaluable book, feel all too familiar to many of us. Whether they come in the form of internal dialogue or come at us from colleagues and bosses, they are deeply disempowering and often leave us feeling very much alone.

But there is good news! You are not alone. Actually, this is both bad and good news. On the one hand, statistics show the prevalence of the above types of doubts and realizations among people of color in response to discriminatory experiences in the workplace. A 2021 study by the Gallup Center on Black Voices found that nearly one in four Black (24%) and Hispanic employees (24%) in the U.S. reported having been discriminated against at work in the previous year.[1] Indeed, race discrimination claims are the most commonly filed cases brought to the Equal Employment Opportunity Commission (EEOC) each year. Yet, paradoxically and unjustly, these claims have the lowest rate of success, with only around 15% of complainants receiving any form of relief or compensation. The nonprofit Center for Public Integrity examined hundreds of EEOC court cases that occurred between 2010 and 2017 and discovered that the chronically underfunded agency closed most cases without ever determining whether discrimination took place. What is more, employees' attorneys have time and again remarked that EEOC investigations are often not conducted professionally or comprehensively. Sometimes they only involve requesting a response from the employer.[2]

The high occurrence of discrimination against employees of color and the discrepancies in power dynamics in the EEOC process indicate the predominance of patriarchal white supremacist culture that can be devastating to the careers and well-being of people of color in the American workforce. Careers are stymied at all points—hiring, projects and assignments, team staffing, performance reviews, promotion, and pay. On top of this, studies such as sociologist Kathryn Freeman Anderson's "Diagnosing Discrimination: Stress from Perceived Racism and the Mental and Physical Health Effects"[3] and the *American Journal of Public Health* 2012 special issue on "The State of Research on Racial/Ethnic Discrimination in the Receipt of Health Care"[4] have long documented the emotional and physical stress endured by people from underrepresented groups who are subjected to discriminatory environments. Health and wellness outcomes—not to mention careers—in both the short and long term are adversely affected for Black, Latinx, and other minoritized individuals.[5]

It is one thing to reckon with statistics and scientific studies on discrimination, but it is another thing to live through it. The confusion, anger, despair, and isolation can be profoundly demoralizing and even dangerous. Many of us have suffered through innumerable "not-so-micro aggressions," as Brenda Harrington calls them, from their employers, like the comments at the top of this foreword and other backhanded compliments ("You are so articulate!") that Harrington addresses. We then end up trying to process the accompanying types of thoughts and questions also articulated above, wondering what is wrong and where we go from here. All of this can leave us feeling lost and utterly disempowered.

This is where the good news returns in the form of this significant and empowering book. Brenda Harrington, a tremendously successful Black woman business executive, educator, and executive coach, brings to bear her decades of experience and connections in multiple industries to provide people of color with practical tools to take our power back. In nine cogent and illuminating chapters, Harrington offers a comprehensive set of approaches to coping with discrimination and succeeding despite the obstacles we face. Each chapter focuses on examples of lived experiences of people of color in multiple sectors: business, government, technology, higher education, the arts. This makes the book useful to individuals pursuing careers in each of these arenas specifically, but also offers an opportunity to gain enriching insights from forms of discrimination in fields that are different from our own.

Harrington offers vitally important insights regarding phenomena and decision-making that many of us face. How can and should I assimilate into the patriarchal, white-dominated culture of my workplace? How can I crack the cultural and structural code at my job? What are the benefits and risks of such assimilation and the code-switching it requires? How can and should I strengthen relationships with colleagues and bosses in order to bolster my visibility and the appraisal of my work? How much do I really need a network of support and guidance in order to succeed? Who should be a part of my network and how do I go about building it? How do I calibrate my ambitions to progress at my job and in my field?

As Harrington guides us through these critical subjects, she highlights the importance of psychological awareness. This involves an honest exploration of our personal and professional histories and shining light onto our often unarticulated expectations regarding our educational and career prospects, our jobs, and our colleagues. Throughout the book, Harrington puts forward smart and useful questions to scaffold our process of self-examination. In this way, she gives the reader executive coaching—for a fraction of the price—that will give you knowledge and courage to advocate for yourself in the best ways possible.

Ultimately, Brenda Harrington offers us the support that we deserve and too often struggle to find in our educational and career trajectories: empathy, straight talk, mentorship, and camaraderie geared to uplift us and assist us in uplifting ourselves. *Access Denied* is an engaging and transformative read that is more urgent than ever.

Christy Pichichero, PhD (she/her/hers)

Associate Professor of French and History

Director of Faculty Diversity, College of Humanities and Social Sciences

George Mason University

www.christypichichero.com

NOTES

1 Camille Lloyd, "One in Four Black Workers Report Discrimination at Work," Gallup Center on Black Voices, January 12, 2021, https://news.gallup.com/poll/328394/one-four-black-workers-report-discrimination-work.aspx

2 Maryam Jameel and Joe Yerardi, "Workplace discrimination is illegal. But our data shows it's still a huge problem," *Vox*/Center for Public Integrity, February 28, 2019, https://www.vox.com/policy-and-politics/2019/2/28/18241973/workplace-discrimination-cpi-investigation-eeoc

3 Kathryn Freeman Anderson, "Diagnosing Discrimination: Stress from Perceived Racism and the Mental and Physical Health Effects," *Sociological Inquiry* 83, no. 1 (February 2013): 55–81, https://onlinelibrary.wiley.com/doi/abs/10.1111/j.1475-682X.2012.00433.x

4 Vickie L. Shavers, Pebbles Fagan, Dionne Jones, William M. P. Klein, Josephine Boyington, Carmen Moten, and Edward Rorie, "The State of Research on Racial/Ethnic Discrimination in The Receipt of Health Care," *American Journal of Public Health* 102 (2012): 953–966, https://doi.org/10.2105/AJPH.2012.300773

5 Jason Silverstein, "How Racism Is Bad for Our Bodies," *The Atlantic*, March 12, 2013, https://www.theatlantic.com/health/archive/2013/03/how-racism-is-bad-for-our-bodies/273911/

INTRODUCTION

You receive an invitation to a gala, hosted by one of the premier organizations in your field. "Formal attire, cocktails at seven, dinner at eight o'clock." You arrive on time, in an outfit you spent more on than your parents paid for their first house. Once inside, you connect with many of your colleagues and others you know from your industry. Together you enjoy the passed hors d'oeuvres, the crudités and charcuterie, and signature cocktail.

A few minutes before the dinner hour, you hear dinner chimes permeating the chorus of more than two hundred voices, all speaking at once. The time has come for the main event! The crowd begins to file into the ballroom, where everyone is to be seated for an opulent five-course gastronomic experience. As you approach the threshold, one of the event hosts appears, holding his hand up in front of you. "I'm sorry, hors d'oeuvres only for you. Feel free to remain in the reception area for as long as you wish, but I'm afraid you will not be able to join us for dinner." Are my shoes the wrong color? Should I have worn different jewelry? What did I do wrong? There is a good chance that you've done most things right. But when requirements are fluid, the rules discretionary, and politics are at play, it can be almost impossible to crack the code necessary for you to gain entry to the main event. Or is it even possible? What if you were never intended to stay for dinner?

This metaphor inspired by my sister, Yvonne Curtis, depicts the circumstances many people of color face when trying to decode the protocol for achieving workplace acceptance and success. Beyond being educated, having a strong work ethic, good experience, and demonstrated past performance, it is the unwritten, obscure details that are used at the discretion of decision-makers and people in power as barriers to advancement opportunities and positions of greater significance. In many cases, this is not necessarily because a person is not technically qualified or has done something wrong. There are many variables that have nothing to do with a person's education, experience, or accomplishments that will significantly influence his or her standing for higher-level positions and opportunities for advancement. If and when such circumstances are applicable to members of the dominant group, they are often seen as mentoring or learning opportunities for professional development. But when it is one of us, it is used as a nail—and sometimes the last nail in the proverbial professional coffin that leads to a dead end. We've had to place so much focus on having the best qualifications and making sure our work is twice as good; the significance of everything that happens in the background is lost on us. Without access to mentors and organization sponsors who can provide much-needed advice, coaching, and counsel, many of us are not prepared for the real game that is being played. It is as if we are trying to play soccer on a baseball diamond. It won't work. Not being prepared to navigate the political and social organizational landscape—or even knowing it exists—places minorities at a competitive disadvantage. It is far from sufficient to report to work, do great work, and return home. Playing to win requires an understanding of the game, knowing who the star players are, and developing and executing a playing strategy. The most important thing is to set expectations that are grounded in reality.

I wrote this book primarily for people of color—of all ages and at all career stages—seeking better professional opportunities, more senior positions, and in some cases, who just want to be treated equally. Experiences of real people are presented to convey three key messages:

▶ No, you are not crazy. What has happened and is happening to you is real.
▶ You are not alone. What has happened to you has happened and is happening to others.
▶ We cannot change the hearts and minds of those with biases that do not favor us, but we can make choices to better protect and advocate for ourselves and each other.

Stories presented are augmented with reflective questions and exercises to help you assess your own circumstances and develop a strategy and plan to support your ability to achieve your professional goals and what you want for yourself.

THE SCHEMAS WE LIVE BY

This book is an exploration of the schemas that inform how we see ourselves and how others see us. A schema is a cognitive framework or concept that helps organize and interpret information. It helps us to take shortcuts when interpreting large amounts of information in and about our environment. A schema can also cause us to exclude important information that we should focus on, allowing us to yield to the things that confirm our preexisting beliefs and ideas. Through a series of stories, we look at the schemas that inform how we see ourselves, or self-schemas, as well as the schemas that influence how others see us.

Section I is offered to help you consider your self-schema. What are the experiences that have influenced who you are and the way you see yourself? To help you answer this question, I've shared information about my own early life experiences that informed my perception of myself and some of my expectations about how I would be viewed by others. Provided at the end of Chapter 1 are questions to help you consider the path of your own life, the experiences and stories that have impacted you along the way.

As an executive coach, I work with clients of all different cultures, races, and nationalities, with a wide variety of backgrounds. Part of my role as coach is to help clients discover new possibilities for themselves by developing new approaches to their way of being and doing, while setting aside practices and in some cases stories that no longer serve them. Although each client's journey is unique, the distinctly different paths of many people have led them to the same place, and in some cases to facing similar challenges. What changes is each person's unique response to their experiences based on how they see themselves and who they believe themselves to be. My hope is that you will entertain questions provided at the end of the first chapter to help you reflect on your own life experiences, the stories that have the most influence on you and their current relevance.

Section II is an exploration of the schema of prejudice, its impact on beliefs about minoritized groups, and the corroboration of beliefs over adaptation when they are challenged. Through a collection of stories, details of actual experiences are presented to demonstrate the pervasiveness of beliefs that support the subordination of members of minoritized groups. Whether you "see yourself" in a story, or identify circumstances described as a potential reality, I invite you to consider the companion questions and reflective exercises provided with each chapter.

WHAT THIS BOOK IS, AND WHAT IT IS NOT

While I am primarily speaking to people who look like me, this book is a resource for anyone who has ever questioned the equity of experiences in the workplace, even when they may not be directly impacted by them. It is intended to provide people of color and members of minoritized and marginalized groups with tools to navigate their circumstances more effectively. For anyone who identifies as a member of another group, it is an honest and unabridged commentary on what we as minorities experience, how it makes us feel, and the impact our experiences can have on our quality of life.

This book is not a universal indictment of all companies, institutions, and organizations, nor is it intended to suggest that all members of the dominant group commit intentional acts of discrimination. It does, perhaps, share perspectives that some may not have been compelled to consider.

THE SWALLOWTAIL BUTTERFLY

Butterflies, in general, are thought of as symbols of transformation. The swallowtail butterfly is often associated with hope, endurance and change. The broken swallowtail wing as conceptualized by our illustrator accompanies each story as an acknowledgment of hopes that were diminished, endurance that was tested, and the absence of change that is long overdue.

SECTION I

THE IMPACT OF EARLY EXPERIENCES

Access Denied

14

Chapter I

Identity and Our
Perception of Ourselves

Our sense of who we are and who we can become is formed over time. Beginning with our early childhood experiences, we develop a sense of our being based on our surroundings, the people in our lives, our relationships, and a host of other factors. Over time, new experiences inform our development, perhaps the evolution of how we see ourselves and who we are in relation to the rest of the world.

The following path of my life is offered as a frame to help you think about the early stages of your own life, the formation of your values, and who you are today. The exercise at the end of this chapter will provide additional scaffolding intended to help affirm the origin of your aspirations, your beliefs about who you are, and what you want.

I grew up next door to a synagogue. On many occasions during my pre-school years, I recall being invited to play with the children attending Hebrew school when they were outside for recess. When they spotted me on the other side of the chain-link fence playing alone on my swing set, their teacher would invite me to come over to play with them. I would join them for a few rounds of Ring Around the Rosie with my mother's permission. That was the extent of our interaction, but I always felt welcomed and accepted. If there were differences between us other than our skin color, it was not apparent to me at the time.

Fast-forward to the morning of my seventh birthday, a school day. I asked my mother if I could wear my hair "out" for the day. This was our way of referring to hair that was not braided or twisted. Mommy agreed, and we proceeded to the kitchen to put the hot comb on the stove so that she could smooth my edges, just as she would on Sunday before church or when getting me ready for a special occasion. She placed a barrette or two on the sides, and off I went! I remember feeling more like other girls in my class whose hair I had never seen in braids at all. It was a good day, until my teacher sent me home with a note in an envelope pinned to my dress. When I arrived home, I learned that the note was a request to my mother not to allow me to come to school with my hair not in braids because it was too distracting. I recall feeling like I was in trouble, but I hadn't done anything wrong. This is my earliest memory of being called out because of a difference between myself and others. But at the time, I did not understand why or what it meant.

It was the 1960s, Mount Vernon, New York. Our parents were extremely proud of the home they purchased in a mixed neighborhood. They wanted the best for my sister and me, always telling us that we could be anything we wanted to be in life. I do not recall our having conversations about race, and certainly did not speak in terms of being a negro as something that would be a limitation for us. Looking back on it now, we seemed to exist in an us/them reality that today we might describe as everyone staying in their lane. With all due respect, our parents seemed to be buying into the idea that progress was being made and that society was moving beyond the racial indiscretions of the past toward equality. If my sister and I focused on education and worked hard, anything would be possible for us. The civil rights movement was in high gear, but what little we knew about what was happening "down south" seemed to be a world away.

News about the "movement" was limited, overshadowed significantly by reporting on the Vietnam War. And although the 1965 assassination of Malcolm X took place in the Bronx, just 12.4 miles from our front door, I don't recall being aware of what that meant until I met his daughter, Attallah Shabazz, a few years later while I was a student at Minnie S. Graham Elementary School. Regardless of the conversations that did or did not occur at home, my awareness significantly increased the afternoon of April 4, 1968, with news of the assassination of Dr. Martin Luther King Jr.

EARLY AWARENESS

I was watching television in my parents' bedroom; they were having a conversation in the kitchen downstairs. Whatever I was watching was interrupted by a news report that Dr. Martin Luther King Jr. had been shot and killed. I immediately ran downstairs to tell my parents what I heard. Their initial reaction was that I must have been mistaken, until they turned on the television to hear the news for themselves. They responded with sadness and disbelief. At that moment, there was suddenly a stronger connection between our family and the community that previously seemed so distant as we processed the devastating loss of the person we all believed would lead the way toward a brighter future, away from what we knew to be a dark past.

Around that time, my sister was experiencing the impact of a direct act of discrimination committed by her guidance counselor at Mount Vernon High School. Yvonne always wanted to be a nurse. Her first job as a teenager was as a member of the kitchen staff at Mount Vernon Hospital, where she delivered meals to patients. This was her way of getting to know the hospital and medical environment. It would appear that her high school guidance counselor had other ideas. She discouraged Yvonne from attending college, suggesting that if wearing a white uniform was the attraction she could work in catering or become a hair dresser. The counselor did not even help Yvonne select the requisite biology and chemistry classes required for nursing school acceptance, suggesting that the course work would be too difficult for her. Becoming aware of the prerequisites she would need *after* graduating from high school, Yvonne enrolled in summer school on her own to complete the courses needed to fulfill admission requirements. In 1971, she graduated from Pace University (Pace College at that time) as a Registered Nurse (RN).

By that time, I was a junior high school student at the Mt. Vernon High School Annex. I took advantage of the opportunity to pay that same counselor a visit, presenting her with Yvonne's graduation picture from Pace College School of Nursing, wearing her black banded cap. In those days, RNs wore white caps with black bands which distinguished them from other members of the medical profession. I reminded the counselor of the conversations she had with Yvonne years earlier, letting her know that despite her discouraging words, my sister prevailed! Yvonne would later tell me about conversations she had during class reunions with other Black classmates who also recounted stories of being discouraged by educators from pursuing higher education and being directed to vocational training and trade school.

When I was in junior high school in the early 1970s, our family moved 13 miles north to the Greenburgh section of White Plains, New York, to shorten my father's commute to work. Now, as a student at Woodlands High School, I began experiencing complexities involving race that were very different from anything I had encountered in Mount Vernon. There were fractures that created a dynamic of disharmony within the Black community: where you lived, the occupation of your parents, and their level of education, to name a few. High-highs and low-lows bracketed the socio-economic spectrum for members of the Black community. Among residents of the Black community in Greenburgh were comedian Moms Mabley and baseball legend Roy Campanella. What was very different for me was the type of social camaraderie that existed among Black and white students, especially around athletics. Although there wasn't a great deal of overt racial tension in Mount Vernon, there wasn't the degree of social interaction between members of the Black and white community that existed here. Social dynamics aside, there was a clear message that the road to success was paved with a good education, learning how to work with others, and gaining new experiences (emphasized through involvement with sports and student and community activities). There were members of the Black community who achieved prominence as educators in Greenburgh Central School District as teachers, guidance counselors, and school board members, who were also very visible in the community at large. There was also a Black fire commissioner, and minorities in other disciplines that helped us see some of the possibilities that existed for us. I realized that what we were living was way more complex than Black vs. white, and a reckoning with the past. It was clear that these people weren't waiting for permission or to be told what they could or could not do. They had figured out a way to coexist, and in some cases, thrive in a system developed and controlled by the dominant group.

Following my sister's experience with high school guidance counseling, I decided to practice greater self-advocacy when it was my turn to focus on post-secondary education. As a sophomore planning my academic schedule for the last two years, it became clear that I would have only two required classes and a great deal of free time by senior year. With the support of my counselor and my parents, I doubled up on English and Social Studies in my junior year and graduated one year early. For me, pulling this off was proof positive that the messaging received from my parents all my life was true: if I could see it, I could do it, and I could be it! Off to college I went!

DEVELOPING A SENSE OF SELF

Many things inform our self-perceptions and identity as teenagers, not the least of which is how we see ourselves relative to others. In addition to our personal identity, we also develop a social identity based on being part of various groups: our family and ethnicity, for example. In addition to self-identification, the groups we belong to help others to identify us.

Erik Erikson has most extensively described identity formation in his theory of developmental stages, which extends from birth through adulthood. According to Erikson, identity formation, while beginning in childhood, gains prominence during adolescence. Faced with physical growth, sexual maturation, and impending career choices, adolescents must accomplish the task of integrating their prior experiences and characteristics into a stable identity. Erikson coined the phrase "identity crisis" to describe the temporary instability and confusion adolescents experience as they struggle with alternatives and choices. To cope with the uncertainties of this stage, adolescents may overidentify with heroes and mentors, fall in love, and bond together in cliques, excluding others based on real or imagined differences.

When it was time for me to go to college, I had a good sense of whom I did and did not want to be. I wanted to be someone who could achieve goals and experience self-defined success. I realized many things that were important to others were not important to me and, in some cases, did not matter to me at all. Although I enjoyed having friends and being around other people, I did not feel a need to conform or seek the approval of others. Uniqueness was something I valued, and independence of thought was a priority. The achievement of graduating early from high school helped me to become comfortable with speaking up and taking risks. I did not want to be someone closely controlled by formalities and processes set in motion at the pleasure and for the convenience of others. It was important to me to maintain a modicum of freedom and control my circumstances.

When you think about the early experiences in your life, what was important to you? How did you make meaning of your environment, what was happening around you, and how it related to what you wanted for yourself in the years ahead? Following is a series of questions to help you reflect on the path of your life and how early experiences have influenced you over time.

THE PATH OF YOUR LIFE

Take time to reflect on your own life stories and what is important to you.

1. When thinking about your earliest memories, what stands out for you?

2. What do those stand-out memories represent?

3. How have those memories influenced the person you've become?

4. What values are represented?

5. How have your earliest experiences helped or hindered your response to challenges you've faced over time?

6. What other questions show up for you?

Chapter 2

The Imprint of
Early Experiences

As a 16-year-old college freshman, the farthest I could get away from home was 35 miles. Adelphi University is a small private school nestled in the affluent New York suburb of Garden City on Long Island. Most of the undergraduate student body was composed of commuters. I was part of the small population of about 1,000 students who lived on campus, a large percentage of whom were people of color. In addition to Black/African American students, we enjoyed a significant number of Hispanic students and students from the Caribbean. I was fascinated that such a diverse group of people found their way to a small school tucked away in a wealthy Nassau County community. For the most part, the campus was our safe place, but the surrounding community was less than welcoming. I recall feeling like a bit of a leper when venturing out to shop or use neighborhood services. It was not uncommon to be ignored by merchants and shop owners along Nassau Blvd. While I was never denied service, it was apparent that they would not have been disappointed with my conducting business elsewhere.

The Long Island Railroad (LIRR), Stewart Avenue stop provided public transportation access to Adelphi. I did not use LIRR but can recall several accounts of Black students being stopped and questioned by police on the way to and from the train station about why they were in the neighborhood. At the time, I could not have imagined what a metaphor all of this would be for the years to come. The very good thing was that those of us who lived on campus were like one big extended family. Even if we didn't know each other personally, we knew of each other and looked out for each other in an almost sibling kind of way. When we found ourselves in classes together, we would do what we could to support each other academically. During this time, that meant studying together, sharing, and comparing notes and, at times, textbooks, helping each other prepare term papers and assignments, especially preparing for midterm and final exams. It was not uncommon for many of us to have to balance on/off-campus employment with academic responsibilities, which sometimes resulted in schedule conflicts and, from time to time, just plain fatigue.

Adelphi University is where I discovered Alpha Kappa Alpha Sorority Inc. (AKA). I was the fourth on a pledge line of ten, initiated in December 1976. We were one of two Divine Nine organizations on campus, side-by-side with the brothers of Alpha Phi Alpha Fraternity Inc.

Being members of Black Greek-letter organizations in a small, predominantly white campus community took whatever racial divide distinction existed to a whole new level. As members of AKA, we were focused on community service and programs driven by our larger, predominantly adult/graduate-membership organization focused on national and international social challenges—service to all mankind. Other sororities on campus appeared to have different priorities. This created a dynamic that would at times strain our relationship with the other organizations with which we had to share university-designated space for Greek-letter organizations, the Panhellenic Suite. There were more of them than there were of us, and we had to be resolute in standing our ground to protect our interests. We also learned how to work together effectively as a group, developing skills I am sure many of us have called on over the course of our professional lives. I reflect on this period with profound gratitude for the metaphor it would be for years to come, and especially for the durable relationships among "sister friends" that have stood the test of time.

Many of us who became AKAs at Adelphi remain in very close contact more than forty years later. We reminisced about some of our early experiences during one of our many Zoom calls together, juxtaposing them with current events. One of our sorors reflected on a 1977 conversation with her academic advisor when preparing to apply to the PhD program at Adelphi's Derner School of Psychology.

Dr. Marjorie Hill is an experienced nonprofit executive with extensive expertise in health management, diversity and inclusion, and HIV/AIDS. A licensed clinical psychologist, Dr. Hill's portfolio of consultant services includes nonprofit agency sustainability, board engagement, conflict resolution, and executive coaching. But this might not have come to pass if Marjorie had followed the advice of her academic advisor upon her arrival at Adelphi.

Story 1

You Should Try Something Else

I n the summer between 10th and 11th grade, I decided I wanted to become a psychologist. To my knowledge, there were no mental health professionals in my family, and no one had yet attended graduate school. At that time, neither of my parents had attended college. My mother went to college at night after I graduated from high school and obtained a BA in 1982.

As I began the task of college selection, my mother arranged a meeting with one of her advisors at the New York Technical College, a two-year institution that was part of the City

University of New York (CUNY) system. This advisor was not a psychologist, but was extremely knowledgeable about CUNY and college success. He strongly recommended that I apply to Staten Island Community College and major in Liberal Arts because it was the best two-year college in the system. Liberal Arts would best prepare me for psychology or another major should I change my mind. Excelling at SICC would also heighten my profile when (and if) I applied to a four-year institution. I accepted his advice and subsequently graduated from SICC with honors.

My decision to apply to Adelphi University was a very easy and straightforward one. Liberal Arts concentration had confirmed my interest in psychology. Adelphi had a solid undergraduate psychology program, but it was the graduate school that I was determined to attend. Adelphi's Institute of Advanced Psychological Studies was rated one of the top clinical psychology programs in the nation. My plan was to attend Adelphi as an undergraduate, graduate with honors, apply, and get accepted into the Institute.

I was thrilled upon receiving my Adelphi acceptance letter. I identified some preliminary psychology courses and scheduled the required meeting with my assigned Psychology Department advisor. I was so excited about finally having the opportunity to review my plan and share my dream with someone who had academic psychology expertise. The advisor reviewed my transcript, approved my course selection, and inquired about my career plans. I excitedly shared that I wanted to become a clinical psychologist and planned to apply to Adelphi's graduate program. "The Institute is a highly competitive program, receiv-

ing 500 or more applications for the 25 slots," she replied. "You should try something else."

To this day, I cannot recall anything beyond those words. What I said or did. I do recall being painfully stunned. That was the fall of 1975. I never scheduled another meeting with her, nor can I recall whether she attempted to reach out to me. I was determined not to let my dream be deferred. A highly motivated, intelligent, resilient young woman, with the support of my family, church, and Black psychology professionals I met through this journey—I persevered. Approximately 18 months later, in the spring of 1977, I returned to the advisor's office. I placed a copy of my Institute of Advanced Psychological Studies acceptance letter on her desk. Good thing I did not try "something else." Head held high; I walked out of her office. I was the youngest student in my 25-person class and the first to be conferred with a PhD.

If this sounds familiar, it may be because of its similarity to the issue involving educational counseling that took place a decade earlier. I, for one, am grateful that Marjorie (Dr. Hill) did NOT follow the guidance of her advisor, the very person whose job it was to help students develop their academic and professional aspirations. Listening to Marjorie's story made me begin to think of these not-so-micro aggressions in terms of ten-year markers. Were they still happening in 1987? In '97? Surely not into the 21st century—or are they? It occurred to me that I could personally check the box for 1987 with an experience detailed in the next chapter.

FINDING YOUR CHEERING SECTION

As Dr. Hill mentioned, it was her vast support system that helped her to remain focused and stay on track. Unfortunately, we cannot always rely on those designated to act in our best interests to do what is best for us, especially when it conflicts with their personal beliefs and values. The absence of encouragement and support from family, friends, and loved ones is what can allow space for reservations, second-guessing, and our inner saboteurs to affect us. In the workplace, not having mentors and sponsors can make the grade of an uphill climb feel even steeper when you're trying to discern how much of what you are experiencing represents truth and reality, and to what extent you are being impacted by personal bias and discrimination.

Discouragement in any form may have nothing to do with you, your capabilities, or what you can achieve. When you hear "no," it often means the answer could be "absolutely—YES!" During these times, you need a support system of people who will tell you the truth and offer the support you need to move forward. The important thing is to identify people who want you to achieve your goals, and who are willing to provide honest, constructive feedback and input no matter what, and who will coach you along the way.

If you are active in the world of work, it is never too early or too late to identify mentors, to convene a personal team of advisors. Many people think of mentorship as a one-on-one relationship between two people. For countless reasons, it is worthwhile having a series of people to rely on for advice and for the opportunity to talk through challenges as they arise. Given the complex and dynamic nature of the modern work environment, it is not realistic for any one person to be able to effectively address the myriad of challenges that can and will arise.

QUESTIONS TO CONSIDER WHEN IDENTIFYING POTENTIAL MENTORS AND CREATING AN ADVISORY TEAM

1. Whose opinion do you value?

2. Who can you trust to tell you the truth, even when it is not what you want to hear?

3. Who has achieved things you want to accomplish for yourself?

4. Who has insights into your specific discipline or profession?

5. Who in your circle may not be the best mentor or source of advice for you at this time?

Access Denied

34

SECTION II

ENTERING THE
WORLD OF WORK

Access Denied

Chapter 3

Welcome to Corporate Life

M y first real job after graduating from college was with Mobil Oil Corporation. It was an entry-level management position, and my training assignment was at a field location in East Boston, Massachusetts. I lived in corporate housing provided by the company for the duration of my six-month assignment. What an opportunity this was for a recent college graduate entering the professional workforce—at least I thought. At the time, Boston had a long-standing reputation for being among the most racially divided, segregated cities in the United States. Little did I know that East Boston and the corporate housing location in Revere, Massachusetts, were areas that Black people were encouraged to avoid. But there I was, a single, 20-year-old Black woman living alone, working in an environment of racial intolerance. The people both in and out of the office who "looked like me" were not managers, so my interaction with them was frowned upon by senior management. I had nothing in common with nor did I feel comfortable with the people identified as my peers. White colleagues resented the fact that I was young and Black with a college degree, hired directly into a management role they felt entitled to because of their tenure. Other Black employees belonged to the union, and even if they wanted to "like" me, as a manager, I was considered an adversary by default. There were multiple schemas at play: managers were not supposed to interact socially with people who were not managers; minorities should not be in management positions; older, long-time employees should not be supervised by young, new employees—oye! My saving grace was my Adelphi classmate, Alphabrother Kenny McGhie, who was attending law school in Boston at the time, and a second Adelphi alumna, Patricia Elam, who was a Boston native living in Roxbury. As if we were still on campus in Garden City, they looked out for me and served as my support system for those six long months.

My initial assessment was that survival in the corporate environment would require me to peel away much of who I was and develop a different persona. Today this would be referred to as code-switching. Education, skills, experience, and aptitude would have little impact on my ability to succeed, and I would need to choose between assimilating or becoming invisible. I remained at Mobil for two years to test my hypothesis. Personal observations and conversations I was having with other Black colleagues seemed to support my theory. Unsure whether what I was experiencing was company-specific or characteristic of corporate life in general, I decided to try working for a different company to see whether my experiences would be any different.

In 1982 I was hired by AT&T. Overall, there was more diversity among peers than there had been in my previous environment, but there was still an expectation to fit into a certain mold. Donning a suit and relaxing my hair was not a big deal, and I tried hard to soften the sometimes sharp edges of my New York accent so that my words ended in "-ing" instead of "-in." There were interesting social divides always needing to be smoothed out, and it would be those of us in the minority who were expected to yield. Even casual chats could be challenging. For example, in conversations about music, references to "the boss" meant Diana Ross for me, while members of the dominant group were referring to Bruce Springsteen.

About two years after working for the company at an office in Springfield, Massachusetts, I relocated to Reston, Virginia, for a new role. I was learning new skills, receiving positive feedback and performance reviews, and had begun to think about whether this was a place where I could develop a long-term career. But to broaden my experience, I needed to have visibility into other areas of the company. One of the objectives established by my manager and me during my annual performance review was for me to begin exploring new opportunities in other departments. A few months later, my manager was promoted and relocated to a different division and geographic location.

Enter our new manager, Ted. During our initial one-on-one, Ted and I agreed that it was time for me to begin working on a transition, pledging his support to help me navigate the system. He decided that I would have more flexibility to schedule interviews and site visits with other parts of the company if I was placed on "special assignment" and relieved of some of my day-to-day responsibilities. We agreed to meet regularly to confer on my continuing duties for the department and discuss progress with the search for a new position. In all of my naïveté at the time, I had no idea I was being placed in front of a train I did not see coming.

Story II

Notes to Myself

Often when reporting to Ted's office for a scheduled meeting, I would arrive to find a dark, empty room, stood up with no explanation or apology. Over time, I began to feel invisible as our communication all but shut down, and the special assignment meant I would eventually spend most days in the office with nothing to do. One day when I arrived at Ted's dark, empty office, I noticed a sheet of paper on the edge of his desk with my name at the top of the page. It was a written outline detailing his plan to terminate me.

The outline started with an acknowledgment of my performance and results: "Performance exceeds 90% threshold ..." It went on to say the decision to remove me from my position was made by him, with concurrence from his boss. "Her lack of contribution was a decision made by higher management (not Brenda)." The outline ended with "Conclusion: If decision is that want individual off the payroll, then no bonus is the first step to make that happen." I made a copy of the outline and left the original on Ted's desk. A few days later, Ted would inform me that I would not be receiving a bonus for the prior year. He went on to let me know he decided to give me an unsatisfactory performance evaluation to substantiate withholding the bonus. Soon to follow was an announcement that a white male employee was being promoted into my now former role.

I was not without challenges in the role. I struggled with some of the tactics we were asked to implement as managers for our teams to generate sales and was beginning to question how much my personal values and integrity would need to be compromised to comply. I was not the only person who had concerns, but while in the position I continued to do my job as Ted's notes acknowledged. We had not discussed performance issues or performance improvement, and receiving an unsatisfactory performance review was a complete surprise. It appeared there was much more at play than an objective evaluation of my work based on documented results.

I stood alone. As I looked up and around, there wasn't anyone I could look to as an advisor or mentor to help me talk through what was happening. This was also when I became aware of the true role of human resources and their allegiance to the company. My conversations with the HR Business Partner only made things worse. At the very least, I expected them to hold my manager accountable for producing documentation to substantiate his actions. Instead, I was shut out and labeled as a poor performer, a condition that was completely unfamiliar to me.

As things continued to unfold, the company announced the availability of a voluntary separation package for employees meeting eligibility requirements. For a variety of reasons, the idea of moving on was becoming appealing to me. Now having had employment experiences with two Fortune 10 corporations, I realized that success would require much more than good work. I wasn't sure how I felt about relinquishing my career and entire being to people like Ted, who were empowered to make arbitrary decisions about my future, and quite frankly, my well-being. As "corporate" as I had become when it came to appearance, business decorum, and other explicit attributes that were required, it was clear that there were far more implicit, and in some cases, obscure demands I wasn't prepared or willing to accept. I recall a conversation I had with Ted's boss, Wayne, during a business social event out of the office that involved alcohol. A few of my colleagues and I were having a conversation with him about a variety of topics. One of my white female counterparts offered a light-hearted comment which made us all laugh. Wayne turned his attention to me and asked, "Why can't you be more like her?"

Following an awkward pause, another colleague started a new conversation, and I walked away. I was not the go-along-to-get-along type. I watched a few Black colleagues sometimes transform before my eyes, adopting personas unrecognizable as themselves to be accepted and "play the game." For me, this felt like a slippery slope. What was wrong with me? If I become this other "character" to resemble my white counterparts more closely, what happens when that is not enough? I became increasingly uncomfortable with the environment and the people in it.

After careful consideration, I decided to raise my hand for voluntary separation. Before making a final decision, I consulted with an attorney to determine what rights would survive the separation agreement and make sure I would not be at risk of forfeiting an ability to address the actions Ted had taken. My last day as an AT&T employee was April 1, 1987. On April 2, I filed a complaint with the Equal Employment Opportunity Commission.

I was excited to begin a new chapter and to be relieved of the pressure of operating with so much uncertainty in an environment devoid of integrity. But the gravity of what I had experienced continued to weigh me down. What had I done that was so wrong? If there was a performance issue, why wasn't I given a chance to address it? Why wasn't anyone willing—better yet, required to—work through it with me? How could one person wield so much unbridled power?

About two years after leaving AT&T, my case was adjudicated by the Human Rights Commission, Fairfax County,

Virginia. There I sat with my attorney across the table from Ted and the attorney representing AT&T. Among the many questions asked of Ted by the investigator, there were a few that stood out in my mind. The commission had secured copies of my personnel file, which contained a series of favorable performance reviews and little else. When asked about documentation to substantiate the unsatisfactory rating that resulted in my bonus being withheld, Ted indicated that he had not written anything down. When asked whether he had sponsored me for a position in another area of the company as he had committed to do, he said he had not, stating that "I didn't think she would fit in." Among the highlights of his testimony was when he said he was looking out for me and was now being made out to look like the bad guy. Massa, p-l-e-a-s-e!!! The absolute highlight of the hearing was when my attorney presented the investigator with the copy of the outline I found in Ted's office. After a cursory review, he presented the document to Ted and the AT&T attorney. Never had I seen the colors of the rainbow replicated in a human being's complexion so vividly. The investigator asked Ted to explain what the document was. He replied, "Notes to myself." At that point, the AT&T attorney leapt to her feet and said, "I think we should discuss a settlement." Game over!

The sensation that came over me at that moment was something indescribable. It was a combination of relief, vindication, validation, sadness, and anger. What became crystal clear was that short of being white and perhaps male, there was nothing I could have done to change what had taken place. Ted had no interest in me, my career development, and certainly not my well-being. I was pleased to have the matter behind me, and even more grateful for the experience. As unfavorable and unpleasant as it had been for me, I felt that I came out of it whole, with clarity about who I was and who I was not willing to be.

Now on the outside, I paid attention to what friends and former colleagues who had committed to a corporate lifestyle were experiencing. Many were buying into living the buppie life at their own peril. Buppie was a term used in the 1980s to refer to a college-educated Black adult, employed in a well-paying profession, living or working in or near a large city (Merriam-Webster). It was the minoritized version of the term yuppie, which was generally used to refer to a young college-educated adult employed in a well-paying profession. One of these things was clearly not like the other. Young Black professionals were college-educated and may have been similarly paid, but in most cases, our lifestyles, access to resources, mentoring, support, and sponsorship were very different from our white counterparts. The challenges many of my friends faced in the name of making a living were at times untenable. Some found themselves impacted by arbitrary decisions made by people who did not look like them, during conversations that did not include them, conducted in places they did not or could not go. It was apparent that there was so much more to pay attention to, perhaps prioritize, than core and technical competencies, relevant experience, and doing good work. In the absence of mentors and sponsors, decoding an organization's culture, politics, and protocol can be daunting. But so often, when we "look up," there isn't anyone who can relate to our challenges, help us to understand our blind spots, and coach us on how to navigate our surroundings. Successfully landing a position in a chosen field or company is just the beginning. Being able to survive and ideally thrive is a far more formidable undertaking.

REFLECTION

1. Who comes with you to work? Who do you leave at home?

2. To what extent do you find it a necessity to code-switch?

3. How much do you avoid or choose not to code-switch?

4. How has this impacted your career and livelihood?

5. When reflecting on your professional experiences, what surprises have shown up for you? What has caught you off guard?

6. When facing challenges at work, who can you talk with to "unpack" your experiences and help you formulate solutions?

7. Who do you "wish" you could talk to about your experiences? Why?

8. What other questions are showing up for you?

Chapter 4

Cracking the Code

C oming to the realization that doing a great job is not enough can be challenging. When you have bought into the idea that hard work pays off, it can be disheartening to realize that not only isn't great work enough, but there is no playbook outlining what you need to do to advance your career. There are countless implicit messages for us to decipher as we traverse a world of work created and controlled by members of the dominant group. Getting to the root cause of what is happening is the first step. In the best of circumstances, we can affect things, although requiring us to change course, and at times make difficult choices and bold moves. In other, perhaps most situations, there are things we cannot change that place us at a significant disadvantage.

If you are asking yourself, "Do I need to step up my political game?" the answer is probably YES! And depending on your environment and your position, playing politics may need to be your primary focus. Your degrees, experience, and competence serve as an entry card. Paving a path to success begins with interpreting organizational culture, understanding what behaviors are tolerated and rewarded (implied and explicit), and who the power players are. So often, I hear people say, "It isn't right," or "That's not fair; it shouldn't be that way." Precious time is wasted condemning systems and people we are powerless to influence or change. Instead, we need to "read the room" and quickly develop a strategy for navigating our environment in a way that will enable us to protect our best interests and protect ourselves. Unless YOUR name is "on the door," it is unlikely you will be able to hold others accountable for their behavior; even less likely that you will influence hearts and minds informed by assumptions, blind spots, and biases that do not favor you, and that in many cases will create obstacles for you. Ceasing to focus on things you cannot control, and redirecting your attention to the things you can, will enable you to navigate and respond to your environment in a more meaningful way, in the context of what is at the core of the challenges you face.

One area that tends to be underestimated is the work we need to do outside of the office. Sometimes the experiences and interactions that can have the greatest impact on career progression take place away from the office, and in some cases, during nonbusiness hours. Yes—I am talking about those recreational and athletic outings, happy hours, and the myriad of social activities we are sometimes expected to participate in when we are part of a business group or team. It is here that relationships are formed and trust is developed well beyond what can be accomplished in a formal business environment. Though work-related, these pseudo-social settings are not regulated by a company code of conduct or an employee handbook. We get to meet our colleagues again for the first time as all of who they are, and they want to get to know us in the same way. Many factors impact our participation in these extracurricular activities, from our degree of interest and desire to personal demands on our time. And although attendance is not an explicit requirement, not participating can have unintended consequences. By not being present, we risk missing out on important conversations that can directly impact our work and working relationships.

VEILED DISCRIMINATORS

Other areas we need to pay close attention to are those elements of our professional identity that members of the dominant group use to issue discretionary demerits. Topping the list is our dexterity with language and communication, especially when it comes to diction, our use of grammar, and standard English. Regardless of aptitude, intellect, or professional prowess, for Black people, the improper use of pronouns and verbs and challenges with pronunciation are used by some to make far-reaching judgments about our capabilities. Many of us have heard what I call the compliment in code—"You are very articulate!" Why wouldn't I be? The idea that someone's expectation of me is to have limited fluency in my native language is an insult. But people who have only gotten to know us through stereotypes and media portrayals are quick to rely on superficial criteria to make far-reaching judgments about our capabilities. For our counterparts in the dominant group, communication challenges are identified as growth opportunities, accepted as personality quirks, or perhaps as a reflection of their culture and where they are from. While at AT&T, I recall a management meeting where we were discussing an upcoming training event. When assigning a task, one of my white male colleagues began a sentence with "ever who." As politely as I could, I said, "Excuse me—did you say ever who?" He went on to say, "Yes. Ever who begins the first session should be the person that …" I was so stunned, I barely heard anything else that was said for the remainder of the conversation. All I could think about was how I would have been perceived had I started a sentence with "ever who."

Speaking nonstandard English while Black often leads to being judged, being labeled a poor communicator, and in some cases being sidelined. With everything else intact, we are at a loss as to why we don't get to give the presentation or communicate with senior managers and key clients. Sadly, these situations are rarely used as coaching and mentoring opportunities. Instead, they become indictable offenses and are used to place limitations on bright and talented individuals with a great deal to offer. Make no mistake, for minorities in the business world, acumen with the English language is used by the dominant group as both a qualifier and a disqualifier. This is an extremely sensitive topic. There have been times, for example, when I've attempted to talk with someone about replacing "her and I" with "she and I," to replace "should have went" with "should have gone," and "should have did" with "should have done"; it is not always well received. My ask is that when someone from the village offers to help you, please let them. Even if it may not feel good at the time, try to accept it as the gift that it is.

There will be acts committed by members of the dominant group that we would never get away with and that will not serve us well. And let's be honest—there are things we "bring to work" that are better left at home. The point is that we all need someone to hold up a mirror for us, or to let us know when we have spinach between our front teeth. When the way you are "showing up" is not quite right, you need to have someone in your corner to help you course correct. Behaviors and circumstances that present coachable moments for some can result in indictable, career-limiting offenses for others. Everyone needs their own self-selected advocate, someone who is on their side.

CREATE YOUR OWN SIGNALING SYSTEM

Some of the best coachable moments are fleeting. Something is said or done that provides the perfect learning opportunity for growth and development. But short of addressing what occurred publicly or in a timely fashion, the moment slips away, and whatever took place continues to happen again and again. On the flip side, people find it awkward to address potential areas of improvement such as grammar and certain types of behavior. Consider coming up with a code word or type of signal that you can share with a trusted advisor. When he or she observes or becomes aware of a situation and would like to give you the gift of feedback, invoking the signal creates awareness for you, and helps set the stage for you and the person you've entrusted to have a constructive, open, and honest conversation about what took place, and the opportunity for improvement. When thinking of a signal, consider something lighthearted and fun, perhaps something that has meaning for you and the person playing the role of advisor. While it might not feel good at the time, honest feedback is truly a gift that keeps on giving.

We've all heard that as people of color, we must work at least twice as hard and be twice as effective as our white counterparts to achieve similar goals. But the work is only part of it. Regardless of how disheveled others around us might be, how limited their dexterity might be with oral and written communication, and how little they follow protocol, know that we generally do not have that luxury. We need to be on our game, on point all the time, but we must first figure out what that means relative to our surroundings. We can't expect to be recognized for good work alone, and we've got to pay close attention to the politics and unwritten rules that inform the culture of our work environment. The double standard is alive and well!

IS THAT RAIN I'M FEELING?

Have you ever seen the back end of a movie set where the production crew tries to mimic precipitation? They use high-velocity fans to create wind and elaborate networks of water hoses to replicate rain. This is what it can feel like when we are fed empty, poorly developed excuses for why we are not, could not be, and will not be "right" for a particular role or opportunity. Many times, the justification and reasons presented to us just don't make sense. You must ask yourself: Have you lost your mind, or do you just think I've lost mine? But what you may want to say is stop peeing on me and telling me it's raining!

What can be hard to discern is how much the circumstances can be attributed to ignorance and naïveté informed by implicit or explicit bias, and how much can be classified as a form of gaslighting.

The term gaslighting became popular following the 1944 movie *Gaslight*, where a man manipulates his wife to make her think she is losing her mind. Since that time, the term has been used to describe subtle, unhealthy manipulative behavior. Someone experiencing gaslighting may feel undermined and will start to feel a lack of trust toward others. Over time, they begin to lose confidence and question their abilities and competence as they look for the truth in what they have been experiencing.

Recently, Dr. Christy Pichichero, Professor of History at George Mason University, coined the term discriminatory gaslighting to describe what she refers to as "insidious psychological manipulation driven by prejudice and pursued for the purposes of discrimination." A biracial Black woman herself, Dr. Pichichero describes gaslighting as the attempt by an abuser to cause an individual or group to fall into self-doubt, question their perceptions of reality, their memory, and their identity to build their own power and diminish resistance on the part of the victim so that the abuse can continue. "Discriminatory gaslighting happens when dominant social groups use these psychological tricks to maintain their power and privilege by sowing self-doubt and dependence in minoritized groups." In an interview with National Public Radio (NPR),[6] Dr. Pichichero recounted personal bouts with impostor syndrome that began with early narratives around her being accepted to Princeton University, an achievement she duly earned. But reactions from white classmates and their parents were unfavorable, culminating in a statement made directly to her by a white boy "through clenched teeth." "You got into Princeton because you are Black." Even with so many noteworthy accomplishments, Dr. Pichichero second-guessed herself for many years before realizing that she was NOT an impostor and that she was deserving of all the things she had worked so hard to achieve. "I had been a victim of an insidious psychological manipulation driven by prejudice and pursued for the purposes of discrimination. And this type of manipulation needed a name."

I am not suggesting that there are active conspiracies implemented to make people question their sanity. I am saying that the actions of members of the dominant group in their effort to maintain power, position, and status often result in circumstances that defy logic and just don't add up. The result is an unfavorable impact on members of minoritized groups and the targets of such actions. We are expected to accept the reality created for us—and like it! The feeling of being gaslighted can be very damaging, especially for people deeply embedded in an ecosystem that commands high achievement. The introduction of self-doubt and the loss of confidence makes it very difficult for a person to perform at his or her best when the stakes are high.

Consider the experiences of a talented engineer who we will call William, with a proven track record in the consumer products industry. Amid leading multiple high visibility projects simultaneously, he begins to be peppered with vague, condescending comments about his work. Never provided with specific details or constructive feedback, he embarked on an odyssey of trial and error to "fix it," only to realize through the admissions of a new manager that there had never been a problem.

NOTES

6   "Imposter Syndrome, Or Something Else? Historian Talks 'Discriminatory Gaslighting,'" NPR, interview by Lulu Garcia-Navarro with Christy Pichichero on Weekend Edition Sunday, May 9, 2021, https://www.npr.org/2021/05/09/995172973/imposter-syndrome-or-something-else-historian-talks-discriminatory-gaslighting.

Story III

What Did I Do?

William had extensive experience with the development of mobile technology devices for more than fifteen years. His professional DNA was present in many of the products used regularly by a vast majority of consumers worldwide. Because of his track record, he was selected to join a team to participate in the development of a new innovation. For a myriad of business reasons, the project was canceled. William was reassigned to work on the next generation of one of the company's most visible product lines. Soon after landing in his new role, all the members of William's team were reassigned, requiring him to rely on dotted-line, matrixed resources to meet formidable design, development, and production deadlines driven by earning and revenue projections.

In this new role, William was a "fresh set of eyes." He began identifying issues with the potential of having an impact on end-user/customer experience. As he proceeded with the new design, he concurrently attempted to rally support to address issues, in many cases the solutions for which would benefit product lines in other areas of the company in addition to the product line he was responsible for. The challenge, in part, was that some of the problems revealed were not new; they were carryovers from earlier versions that had either gone unnoticed or had not been addressed. It was William's first exposure to the lifecycle of this product line, and rather than this "fresh look" being recognized as an advantage, some of his findings were not welcomed because of the potential negative reflection on his predecessors. This, along with the fact that he was working without a team, made the circumstances untenable. The more he worked, the more work he had to get done.

One day, William's manager advised him that senior management was not happy with his performance. When he asked for details, it was suggested that he have a skip-level meeting with his manager's manager. During that conversation, there was no specific reference or challenge to technical competencies or work products. Superficial comments about communication and information sharing were provided, but nothing that could be considered actionable. Leaving the meeting with more questions than answers, William tried to decipher the message and make adjustments to address the perceived concerns. Ultimately, William simultaneously completed the design and delivery of two products on schedule, generating more positive performance metrics than preceding versions achieved.

Soon after the project was completed, William was told that he needed to work on his soft skills. He was reassigned to a new manager and relegated to working on menial technical tasks reminiscent of work he had done much earlier in his career. If management's concerns were genuinely focused on soft skills, no effort was made to provide resources to support William's growth in that area. The assignment of purely technical tasks was an insult and did not place him in a position to address alleged deficiencies. Tantamount to the "jellybeans in the jar" challenge, William passed with flying colors, producing a product component with ZERO deficiencies or areas requiring corrective action. Other than a brief acknowledgment, there was no meaningful recognition of what he had accomplished, only a request that he complete yet another technical feat that was far below his level of technical competency. Adding insult to injury was a consumer complaint that made it to the office of the company's CEO. The complaint involved one of the issues that had been raised by William that was diminished by his manager and had fallen on deaf ears.

For William, it felt like accomplishments that should have been perceived as "wins" were discounted at every turn. Added to the emotional and physical toll was the financial impact of compensation adjustments that accompanied the arbitrary decisions being made about his performance. On countless occasions, he asked the same question that no one was able or willing to answer: "What did I do that was so wrong?" Although his most recent manager attempted to be more forthcoming, it was clear that William's circumstances were being influenced by some off-the-record, behind-the-scenes dynamic that had nothing to do with his capabilities. If, in fact, there were concerns about soft skills, what could have been an opportunity for development and mentoring became an indictment. William's talents and accomplishments ultimately caught the attention of competitors. He found himself entertaining multiple offers from other companies and has now moved on. Unfortunately, the damage has been done, and it will take him some time to recover from the intensity of the emotional abuse inflicted consistently over an extended period.

Next, meet Samantha. Samantha and the team she ultimately led were acknowledged as having significant, unprecedented impact on her organization's top and bottom line. But despite her accomplishments, she was not someone the organization's executive leadership considered a viable candidate for acceptance into their ranks for reasons they were unable or perhaps unwilling to articulate.

Story IV

You Will Never Go Anywhere in This Organization

A young woman, who we will call Samantha, was one year out of college with a bachelor's degree in Business Administration. Although gainfully employed, she was working hard to gain entry into her profession of choice, working hard to be hired by an organization that dominated her chosen field. Following two unsuccessful attempts, the third time around she was hired as an administrative assistant. Feedback she received prior to becoming an employee was that she lacked the requisite experience for the positions she had previously applied for. Once on board, she realized that in at least one other case, a younger person with no experience had been hired for the position she had applied for. In addition to her professional pursuits, Samantha continued to focus on her education by completing two master's degrees while working full-time. With her sights set on particular functions and divisions within the company, she sought opportunities to gain the experience and exposure to the part of the business she thought she would need to advance her career. This included seeking the mentorship of managers within the organization and expressing interest in cross-training and auditing processes so she could learn about her area of interest. She was told what she did not have on more than a few occasions, but no one seemed to be able or willing to articulate how she could gain the experience she would need to get to where she wanted to be.

Following one promotion and other performance wins, Samantha applied for a position in an area of the company she thought would put her a step closer to where she wanted to be. During her interview, the hiring manager asked her a technical question about the position she was applying for. Not having had exposure to that side of the business, she did not know the answer. The manager's response to her was, "You will never go anywhere in this organization." Samantha was devastated! Not wanting to make waves, she did not report the incident, but later mentioned it to someone in human resources, who indicated she should have come forward. "At the time, I did not have the professional maturity to realize it was a problem." Samantha eventually began reporting to a manager who was willing to help her carve out the path she wanted. "Before being assigned to a new manager, I kept hitting a wall. I felt like a child always asking why." The educational requirement for the entry-level role in Samantha's area of interest was a bachelor's degree. At this point, she had two master's degrees and a few years of experience with the firm, but her interests and inquiries were continually dismissed with few details about what she could do to better position herself for the work she really wanted to do. Following a change in Samantha's skip-level manager, she was granted an opportunity to audit the work she had all but begged to be part of, but was told to be discreet and not talk about it.

Over time, Samantha was able to demonstrate her competencies in the professional area she had pursued for so long. Organizational leadership finally took notice. She was ultimately promoted to a senior management role, leading a department that was responsible for more than 60 percent of the organization's top-line revenue. After spending so much time proving that she could excel in the position she once coveted, Samantha felt she had earned the organization's trust and her career would continue on a positive trajectory. She would eventually find herself again navigating challenges that resembled those she had faced as a young associate.

The next likely role for Samantha would have been an executive-level position as an officer, but she again found herself hitting a wall. After all she had accomplished for the organization consistently over time, she was told that it was not the company's practice to promote from within to executive-level positions. It would only be necessary to map the career of one member of the executive team to dispel that story. Facing excuse after excuse, Samantha again began experiencing the same type of rejection she experienced early on, only this time it felt like a debt that was past due.

A few years ago, I was engaged by Samantha's employer to be her executive coach. When I asked what they wanted us to focus on, I was told they wanted Samantha to improve her executive presence. While they extolled her work and the results she and her team produced consistently, and over a long period of time, they still did not feel she was ready to represent the organization in a top leadership role. Among the concerns they articulated were that she would eat a muffin during management meetings, and they did not feel her attire was as conservative as they would like. Question: Has anyone had this conversation with Samantha? Answer: No. The organization capitalized on Samantha's professional competencies and talents, but little consideration was given to her personal growth and professional development. Despite the great work she was doing, and the exceptional results generated by her department under her leadership, the message being sent to Samantha was that SHE was not enough.

Chapter 5

Names and Faces

For many years we've debated the impact that names can have on first impressions, and even on a person's ability to achieve success in an environment considered homogeneous. Names unfamiliar to the dominant group or those spelled unconventionally can be an issue; when they precede us, they can provide a head start for those who subscribe to superficial judgment to limit diversity. But what happens when our name is a kind of decoy that doesn't align with who people think we are or expect us to be? This can be especially challenging when we find ourselves in transition while seeking employment or new business opportunities. Countless are the times that members of the dominant group—who I would classify as allies—have introduced me to business associates to discuss my services. I can see that they check me out on LinkedIn and other places, but I never hear from them. Here are a few examples of how putting a name with a face is not always a good thing.

Over the years, the name Harrington has certainly thrown people off, revealing biases and racist truths not intended to be shared—at least with me. Before the days of the Internet, when people could not Google you, many assumed I was Irish. On one occasion during my employee relocation days, I was trying to place a brokerage referral for a client considering a move to Scottsdale, Arizona. During a telephone conversation with the Scottsdale broker, I explained that my client was also considering Florida. The broker proudly let me know that if my client liked Florida, they would LOVE Arizona. "We don't have the problems they have in Florida, and we don't have Blacks or Hispanics, so we don't have the political problems that they have in Florida." I was happy to let her talk herself out before reporting her to the Arizona Department of Real Estate.

More egregious than blanket biases about minoritized groups is the notion that a Black person could possibly have the requisite experience and qualifications required to do meaningful work. Hear from two contributors about how the synching of their names and faces led to unfavorable outcomes, even when experience and competency had been demonstrated.

Elena Anderson-de Lay is a highly experienced Global Workforce Mobility professional, fluent in all aspects of visa and immigration requirements. She has served as the lifeline for countless expatriates and their families relocating to and from the United States, ensuring compliance requirements were met and helping them begin life in a new country. Unfortunately, the surprise of her identity would often change the tenor of relationships that had previously been established based on her competency, credentials, compassion, and commitment.

Story V

The Trusted Advisor

From the corner of my eye, I could see him staring at the nameplate on the door. He would look at a sheet of paper, then look at the nameplate. Nameplate, paper ... paper, nameplate. It was a bit comical at first, but it went on for a few minutes. I decided to turn around fully and say, "Hi! Yes, I'm Elena." He looked a bit shocked and actually said, "You are not exactly what I expected." With a smile I said, "I know," and still welcomed him to the organization.

We were meeting together in person for the first time after more than four months of correspondence. We had dozens of email exchanges and several phone calls. You see, Dr. Hui (that's the name we will call him) was a new employee with my organization, and I had guided him through the visa application and acquisition process. He had studied in the U.S. before, but returning as an employee was quite different for him.

When my colleague in human resources notified me of Dr. Hui's job offer, I was told that he wanted to speak with someone about the visa process right away. A conference call was arranged with him, and his soon-to-be director and I talked about the process and the documents I would need from him, while assuring him that I would be his contact through the process. Dr. Hui greatly appreciated the conversation and referred to me as his trusted advisor.

Our initial conversation was followed up by an email memorializing the steps that I referenced earlier. Dr. Hui's case was pretty standard for me as I had been working on academic and employment-based immigration cases since graduating from college. After working in the field for more than ten years, transitions like Dr. Hui's were very familiar to me, but never routine. When working on a colleague's immigration case, you learn a great deal about their lives. Beyond their date and place of birth, you learn about their education and career, and their wedding date.

In some cases, you learn about their divorce date, the births of their children, and other personal details. You even learn about their struggles, anxiety triggers, and even information about their future dreams. By the time you meet them in person, they already feel like a close friend. I usually open up about myself, too, sharing information about my experience growing up in Alabama and how I got into immigration and landed in Washington, DC. Between the emails, phone calls, and courier shipments with their paperwork, I build trust with my future colleagues. By the time they meet me in person, there is an understanding that I am their safe space within the organization, especially as they navigate the organizational culture and the broader culture of Washington, DC.

Shortly after 5:30 one evening, Dr. Hui came to my office unannounced. He had received his first paycheck and was upset about the impact of deductions and the resulting net compensation. Dr. Hui accused me of taking his money. He did not understand FICA or even the pre-tax insurance withholding that he opted-in for with payroll. Apparently, he was in such shock about a Black woman working on his visa documents that he did not hear me warn him about tax withholding during our earlier conversations. It is my practice to meet with my international colleagues first during their onboarding process to explain that working in the U.S. involves layers of taxes and other withholdings that they would not have been impacted by as students. Dr. Hui felt that because there was a treaty with his country, there should be no taxes at all—especially at the state level. "No, that is not how it works," I started to explain. "There are specific provisions in your country's treaty … blah … blah … blah … Let's look together." As I grabbed my binder of treaties, Dr. Hui moved very close to me, into my personal space, and demanded that I give him his money back.

My supervisor and a few other colleagues were still in the office and could hear him yelling at me, but no one came to check on me or stop by my office for support. I stood up, and since we were about the same height, I could look directly into his eyes. I told him to contact the IRS if he wanted his money back. "I don't process payroll, but most of all, I don't steal." We were standing so close to each other that our noses almost touched. I did not know whether Dr. Hui would hit or grab me, and I will never forget how his eyes trembled with anger and how clenched his jaw was. I could feel myself wanting to go into street mode and proactively push him away. But despite his aggressive posture, I still offered to explain why his check had withholdings. He did not say anything for a few seconds, which felt like an eternity. Finally, he let out a big exhale. His hot breath hit my face, then he clenched his fists and stormed out of my office. A few seconds later, my supervisor called my phone. I picked up the phone, still standing in the same position to hear her anxious voice ask, "Are you okay? Do I need to call security?" It is important to point out that her office was close enough that she could have just called out to me. I told her I was not okay, but there was no need to call security. I quietly packed up my things and went home for the day.

Most of my international colleagues do not find out that I am a Black woman until they meet me in person. For years, I had strategically hidden my face from my LinkedIn profile and on other pages that would appear in a Google search. Hiding my face worked out better for me when applying for jobs or leadership positions within my professional associations. I also did not reference my sorority, my place of worship, or any minority-serving organizations on my public profiles so that any potential employers or colleagues would not figure out that I was Black until I had the position. There are not many Black women—especially younger ones—who do the work that I do. Early in my career, I found it exhausting to continuously answer the same qualifying questions: Why are YOU in the immigration field, or how did YOU get this job? I thought hiding part of my identity would help me to be recognized as knowledgeable. The reality *is that it just deferred the shock and inevitability of being asked uncomfortable questions.*

Many of my international colleagues were relieved when they met me in person. When they would look at me and the name-plate on my door, they would let out a sigh of relief, opening up about how their consular process seemed very biased against them, or how certain people would stare and assume they were a jihadist. "I know YOU get what I am talking about" would be a commonplace of connection and understanding between us. But then there is Dr. Hui. I know Hui is a Chinese name, but understand that there were Dr. Huis from every continent. About a third of my international colleagues fit this archetype. They would have an expression of shock when meeting me for the first time, and I would immediately devolve from being their trusted advisor to this impostor pretending to know about immigration. So instead of having a conversation about forms, regulations, and settling in, we would cycle back to a series of uncomfortable questions.

"Where were you educated again? How long have you been doing this work?" Now they are saying it directly to my face. I would respond to their questions and patiently sit through the mumbles and grumbles of "OK, that actually is a good school" and the eye rolls when I would remind them how long I had been doing this work and had been employed by the organiza-tion. Any regulatory information would need to be printed out, as well as their tax treaties, with the provisions highlighted.

In many cases, I had to have colleagues sit in with me to confirm the validity of the information I was providing. The additional work of reprinting and reconfirming the facts often required me to work later than most. I even took work home with me to stay on top of the additional requests and to anticipate new ones. The federal government rarely had inquiries tying back to my work, but I had to work constantly to earn the status of trusted advisor with my colleagues.

When you see, or hear a name like Joy Allen, it doesn't necessarily provide any hints about race or ethnicity. So imagine the potential for surprise reactions when the person who "shows up" is not who was expected.

Story VI

Stealing My Joy

M *y name, Joy Allen, does not speak to ethnicity, and I don't wake up every day thinking about ethnicity. When seeking professional opportunities, I've allowed my résumé to speak for itself. Because of my experience, I've had success getting calls based on my credentials. There are not many people in the interior design and new home construction industry who look like me, and you would not necessarily be able to determine my race when speaking with me over the phone. Over the years, I have experienced a reaction of surprise when people meet me for the first time, but it is something I've been able to overcome in person once we've been able to spend time together. For as long as I could, I even avoided including a picture on my LinkedIn profile.*

Seeking employment during the pandemic only confirmed my assessment about the impact of race when competing for opportunities in my field. One Saturday evening, I submitted my résumé in response to a position posted on a popular Internet job site. The next day, Sunday, I received a very enthusiastic response, requesting my availability for an interview on Monday.

That Monday, less than 48 hours after submitting my résumé, I had a 45-minute virtual interview with a member of the company's senior leadership on Zoom. At the end of the conversation, he stated that he would follow up with me Thursday—three days later—to schedule conversations with other colleagues, confirm a time to meet in person the next Sunday, and discuss the next steps. Based on the conversation he and I had, I literally thought I had the job when the conversation ended.

After the interview, and now with more context, I went back to the company website to prepare for subsequent discussions. Images and photos on the site did not reflect any diversity but based on the initial conversation and commitments made regarding what would come next, I did not think race would be an issue. Later that week, Thursday would come and go with no communication from the person I spoke with or anyone from the company. The next day I sent a follow-up message, and as politely as I could, expressed continued interest in the position and the company. I never heard from anyone at the company again. I felt as though the person I spoke to was committed to moving forward; perhaps that changed when he spoke with his colleagues. Tantamount to ghosting in a social relationship, this is just one example of a time when I believe the reveal of my identity as a Black female overshadowed my experience when seeking employment.

LESSONS LEARNED

In my experience with coaching clients employed by organizations across various business sectors in an array of disciplines, I can attest that acts and actions that marginalize members of minoritized groups are pervasive. Intentional or otherwise, what you may be experiencing is not your imagination. Continuously having your experience and competency questioned, being second-guessed, overlooked, and ignored by members of the dominant group are all things I see and hear about regularly. I especially hear it from intelligent, competent, talented, credentialed, and accomplished professionals of color who find themselves in places that do not value diversity and inclusion—even when they say they do. Of greater concern is the emergence of self-doubt, and bouts with impostor syndrome that can result from perpetually being made to feel that you don't measure up, don't belong, and just aren't enough.

Eleanor Roosevelt once said, "No one can make you feel inferior without your consent." But constantly being questioned and treated like a child, or as if you don't know what you're doing, can take its toll. Having your work reviewed and double-checked by junior colleagues at the direction of senior management, increased scrutiny by senior management because of baseless concerns that you might have made a mistake when you have done everything just right, not receiving recognition—or even acknowledgment when the results you and your team have generated exceed projections and set new records. It is as though a Black person cannot do good work and achieve positive results. This type of behavior is tantamount to hazing, part of the initiation process associated with pursuing membership in a fraternity or sorority. Being continuously subjected to degradation can have a negative and dangerous impact on health and well-being, including the development of chronic stress.

Stress is the physiological demand placed on the body when we are required to adapt, cope, or adjust. Some stress is essential to keeping us alert, enthusiastic, and engaged. But prolonged or chronic stress can have far-reaching negative consequences. It has been cited for prematurely aging our immune system, enhancing the risk of illness and age-related diseases. The consistent requirement to adapt over time has been found to have a cumulative, adverse effect on health, also referred to as allostatic load. Allostatic load is the cumulative biological burden exacted on the body through perpetual adaptation to physical and emotional stress. It is considered to be a risk factor for several diseases—coronary vascular disease, obesity, diabetes, depression, cognitive impairment, and both inflammatory and autoimmune disorders.

Many people's reaction to work-related stress is to dig deeper, work harder, and do more to try turning things around. It is an effort to address deficiencies that, in many cases, do not exist.

Working harder will not quell subjective opinions and actions steeped in discrimination and unconscious bias. Precious time can be wasted trying to make things right, trying to respond to baseless claims about deficiencies and shortcomings that don't exist. What William experienced at his most recent company was a dynamic he had previously been exposed to at three other companies, although less pronounced. Believing he needed to improve something, he lost a great deal of time before positioning and preparing himself to navigate the real challenges at hand, which involved personal bias, intolerance, and bigotry.

At times like these, it is necessary to wage a strategic, more thorough, and thoughtful response to what is really happening. This only becomes possible when we can view a situation holistically, able to zoom out and see things from a broader, more global perspective.

THE ADVANTAGES OF FORMING AN ADVISORY TEAM

When we are too close to a situation, it can be almost impossible to conduct the type of objective assessment needed to understand what is at play; it is hard to see the forest for the trees. But when you begin receiving signals from your intuition that something is not quite right, it is important to pay attention. Wouldn't it be nice if we could count on decisions being based on merit and people doing "the right thing"? But we can't. When you get the sense that something is not quite right, it is worth assessing what is happening around you sooner rather than later. You want to position yourself to proactively influence narratives that involve or may impact you, and you want to exercise damage control before things go too far. We need to have the eyes and opinions of a third party.

It is at times like these that reliance on a support system is so important. In the form of one or more mentors, advisors, or people we trust, we need people to bounce things off of for second and third opinions. We may also need someone who is willing to hold up a mirror to us so that we are able to see what opportunities exist for us to adjust and perhaps take a different approach.

So, who are the mentors and advisors in your life? Are they aware of the role you want them to play, what you want them to do? Following are a few important considerations to help you narrow the list of people you have identified to play such a meaningful role in your professional life.

1. Select people who represent different professions and points of view.

2. Include at least one person with whom you have disagreed in the past, who sees the world differently than you do, and who will tell you the truth.

3. Formalize the "rules of engagement." Tell them what you want from them and make sure they accept.

4. Permit them to be honest, provided their input is constructive.

5. Include a member of the dominant group as part of your advisory team.

6. Express your gratitude for what you want them to do for you.

One of the most significant advantages of having an advisory team is to avoid wasting time. Many people, including me, have bought into the "not enough" judgments of others. While seeking constructive and helpful feedback to fuel our professional development is important, we can't allow other people to define us.

As confident and self-assured as many may have considered me to be, there have been things I felt were off-limits to me. Perhaps this was part of the protective armor I allowed to form around me as a shield to protect myself from reliving some of the things I had already experienced. You cannot be at risk of drowning if you don't go into the pool.

Nearly twenty years after graduating from college, I began to feel as though I was living in too small a space. I was at a point of wanting more, of needing more. The world had changed significantly, and the pace of change was accelerating. I was beginning to feel limited in what I could accomplish, so I decided to return to pursue a master's degree at Virginia Tech. My journey started with enrollment in a single class. Against the warning of the university's program director, I registered for one of the most challenging core classes offered. I was on my own dime and needed to make the most of my time and resources. Little did I know that the professor, Dr. Michael Olsen, was renowned both as a leading business consultant and for his intensely rigorous teaching style. In ignorant bliss, I pursued the course with all I had, in many ways struggling to brush away the dust that had collected on my study habits and sense of discipline over the two decades since my last experience as a student.

I remember preparing for the midterm, studying nonstop, but still feeling uncertain about my ability to achieve a respectable outcome. While returning the exams, Dr. Olsen explained his grading methodology. He told us that he always included one curveball question, and that the person who had the greatest success with that question received additional credit. Dr. Olsen went on to announce that the person with the best answer to the question was me. After hearing my name, I don't think I heard anything else for the rest of the class. For me, this was a breakthrough like none I had ever experienced. It was the moment I realized that yes, I could do it. Yes, I belonged in that program, and yes, many things were possible for me. In addition to taking three additional courses with Dr. Olsen, he and I became great friends. From that point on, I considered him to be the unofficial chair of my team of advisors until his death in 2012.

I would be remiss if I did not address one area that tends to trip us up regarding the way we view the world and assumptions made about the people around us. I am not suggesting that all our workplace experiences are influenced by race. What concerns me at the other extreme is a large swath of people in minoritized groups who have bought into a belief that the world and workplace are colorless. We all have biases, and they show up in places and in ways we may not expect. It is important to have a mechanism in place that enables us to fact-check, solicit objective opinions, and check ourselves and others to see what is really at play. Know that being educated, having a strong work ethic, and experience are not enough to level the playing field for people of color. Playing politics, leveraging networks, and building relationships, having access to a community and support system is necessary for survival, and is essential to our ability to thrive.

Chapter 6

Expectations and the Psychological Contract

For the most part, we are taught at a young age what it means to be a good person. We learn about the Golden Rule and how important it is to do unto others as you would have them do unto you. Growing up, many of us believe that others have similar values, setting as our default a willingness to give others the benefit of the doubt, even when our intuition may suggest otherwise and circumstances appear to be questionable. Despite what optics might suggest, an assumption that others will do what is right prevails, potentially creating unrealistic expectations for what is possible.

I once had a client who was actively involved with recruiting college graduates for openings at her company. The company "speak" was that they wanted to increase diversity but could not find qualified candidates. Part of the problem was that they only recruited from the Ivies and were opposed to casting a wider net. My client advocated for HR to expand recruiting efforts to include HBCUs in response to the message from leadership. Met with pushback, she began lobbying in an effort to gain peer support. One day when expressing her frustration, she asked, "Don't they see what we see?"

The answer is both yes and no. By means of a simple count, do they see that there are fewer minority new hires than those who represent the dominant group? Yes. Is this a problem for them? Probably not. My client's expectation of others that they would see this inequity as a problem that needed to be addressed was unrealistic. It only served to amplify her anger and what we'll call a passionate approach to addressing the issue that was not serving her best interests or what she wanted to accomplish.

Conditions that offend us, that might make us angry or sad are in abundance! When performance metrics have been exceeded, projects are completed successfully, two jobs have been performed successfully for the price of one, client feedback is positive, and there is qualitative and quantitative evidence of our adding value, then it seems plausible that recognition in some form would follow, right? Not so much. And when this idea establishes the premise for our expectations, we end up being disappointed.

It is essential for us to set expectations that have realistic underpinnings. How closely does what we expect align with our environment and its actors? Given the circumstances and people involved, what is reasonable to expect? Embracing unrealistic expectations can place us at a disadvantage that we cannot always recover from. More importantly, valuable time is wasted that we should be spending to develop a strategy and a plan on how best to navigate our environment to achieve desired results. This work is ours to do, and it is something each of us must do for ourselves. We can't sit back and expect others to act in our best interests or to do the right thing.

OUR RELATIONSHIP WITH THE "F" WORD

When expectations and reality are askew, some common responses when things don't work out by those affected begin with "That's not right," "It shouldn't be that way," "I thought …," "I assumed …" These are indicative of a gap between perceptions and reality. But perhaps one of the most troubling responses is "That's not fair." Merriam-Webster defines the word "fair" as being marked by impartiality and honesty: free from self-interest, prejudice, or favoritism, or conforming with the established rules.

When considering the words used to convey the definition and the inherent bias that is so pervasive in organizational systems, it is not realistic to think that members of the dominant group will always share our point of view about what it means to be fair. Assessing others' points of view regarding elements of fairness is among the greatest opportunities to adjust expectations and adapt our approach, actions, and reactions to experiences—to increase our influence on the outcomes we want.

Evaluating expectations begins with being observant, paying attention, and being willing to accept the things you notice at face value. It is at times like these that our intuition will rarely let us down. We just have to figure out what it is trying to tell us. The first thing we need to do is cleanse our minds and neutralize our thoughts about what should be, or how things might play out under ideal circumstances. Next, we need to think about the data points available to us and what they represent. Things to consider, for example, may involve the relationships and dynamics among colleagues and the people around you. What are the possible scenarios that need to be taken into consideration? When you find yourself thinking about extremes and perhaps saying to yourself, "That could never happen," you are likely touching on something that warrants a closer look. Much like we think about disruption at an organizational level, we must apply a similar thought process when contemplating conditions that could have individual impact. At all costs, it is important to avoid being blindsided.

THE PSYCHOLOGICAL CONTRACT

The term "psychological contract" refers to the expectations individuals have about their employer/employee relationship. Not explicit and only implied, it involves parties' perceptions on both sides about what they stand to receive in exchange for whatever they have committed to providing. In general, the perceptions employees have about their employers' obligations are vague and somewhat dynamic. There was a time that the focus of this "understanding" between employer and employee centered on loyalty in exchange for job security, and today there is an emphasis on career development and compensation. Insights are often based on how employees interpret the words, actions, and deeds of their immediate supervisor or manager, involving both themselves and others.

A good starting point for evaluating the aptness of your expectations is to think about the tenor of the psychological contract between your employer and the people who work there in general. You may then want to ask yourself a few simple questions: How do my expectations align with what I see and hear happening around me? Based on what I know, are my expectations realistic? What, if anything, can I do to influence outcomes so that my expectations are met? Be sure not to think about your circumstances in isolation. For example, "I've done more work than others," "I have more experience," and "I've been here the longest" do not provide a meaningful premise for establishing expectations. Much like scenario and strategic planning exercises conducted to anticipate business outcomes, it helps to apply similar methods and concepts to your professional experiences with colleagues and managers, as well as people who report up to you. Know that there is no refuge in the contours of what we may perceive to be fair, only expectations that may impede our ability to achieve realistic outcomes.

In the summer of 2018, Dr. Jeanette Kowalik, PhD, MPH, MCHES, was selected to be the next Commissioner of Health in her hometown of Milwaukee, Wisconsin. For her, it was a lifelong dream come true. Despite the red flags that popped up along the way, Dr. Kowalik proceeded on a course inspired, at least in part, by the idea that she would now lead the same health department where she started her public health career as an intern. The obligation she felt to her city and the department she "grew up in" did not always support alignment between her expectations and the reality of what was possible.

Story VII

Welcome Home

M y journey back to Milwaukee was a rocky one. The "growing up in public health experience," which I thought would be a good thing, ended up having an adverse impact in two key areas: First, there were people who still viewed and treated me like an intern. Second, I had a number of relationships with staff going back to my time as an intern that were not as durable as I would have hoped and did not last. Because I'd worked in other settings, I had grown and evolved professionally in a way that others had not; it was as if it was 2008 all over again. This dynamic was the source of added complexity, resulting in the loss *of colleagues and friends I counted on for support. I held many people in very high regard, only to find out that we had different values regarding impartiality and fairness. I found myself grieving many losses, but only in part because I was so committed to "fixing the department."*

One of my main priorities as commissioner was to address racism and health equity. As a Black Polish Milwaukeean, I experienced racism and segregation regularly. I was born and raised in Sherman Park, one of Milwaukee's leading areas for negative health outcomes and poverty. I was grateful for the work I had done as the University of Wisconsin's Health Officer, and in Washington, DC, as the Associate Director of Women's and Infant Health for the Association of Maternal and Child Health Programs (AMCHP). Both equipped me with the systems, language, knowledge, and relationships to ensure Milwaukee would take the first steps toward declaring racism a public health crisis.

Milwaukee County made the racism declaration first in May 2019. At the city level, we were able to do the same in July 2019,[7] noting that Milwaukee City and County would be the first in the United States to do so. In addition to reorganizing and fixing the very department that was responsible for my public health career, we began the work of the anti-racism declaration. The first action item was to complete a needs assessment with the Equal Rights Commission. This coincided with preparation for the Democratic National Convention (summer 2020) and the coronavirus pandemic.

Like so many others, my priorities shifted entirely on March 13, 2020, when our first city and county COVID-19 case

89

was detected. Due to the County Executive's emergency orders, I became responsible for the pandemic response for both the city and county, totaling more than one million people. Daily media briefings, politics, and egos took precedence over best interests. Among our most significant challenges was the difference in philosophy regarding public health orders between the city and some suburban leaders in the county who represented white, more affluent constituents. The pandemic magnified race-related disparities, and it was our priority to protect the community as a whole. We were required to operate as part of a Unified Emergency Operations Center (UEOC). I constantly had to advocate for myself, my team, and our community. There was one white female who decided she needed to call all of the shots. She blocked me by not sharing information or respecting my decision-making authority and would hold meetings without me. She refused to acknowledge staff members from the City of Milwaukee assigned to the UEOC because we did not support her point of view. With the highest rate of poverty and the most diverse populace in the state, we felt it was important to issue public health orders that were enforceable by law, while our counterparts in the suburbs opted to issue recommendations and guidelines that were not enforceable. The City of Milwaukee's position on orders created a rift between businesses across city limits; those outside of the city saw increases in business because they resumed in-person activities while the city did not, due to the orders. As part of our effort to implement manageable and responsible solutions, we turned to Race Forward's guidance for equitable policies. Race Forward is a social justice organization that brings systemic analysis and an innovative approach to complex race issues to help people take effective action toward racial equity. Based on their guidance, we developed a mask ordinance that focused on businesses—to reduce inequality in citations—instead of individuals.

Saving lives was the premise for everything I wanted to accomplish as Health Commissioner, and I had to come to the difficult realization that others in my field did not share my priorities. Expecting support for initiatives focused on racism and health equity was unrealistic, especially in the shadow of affluent constituents' political and economic interests.

Evaluating Your Expectations

1. What do my expectations represent?

2. How closely do my expectations reflect my values?

91

3. What is most important to me, and why?

4. Are my expectations realistic?

5. Are my expectations aligned with my work environment and the actors involved?

6. Do my expectations represent what I want for myself, or others' expectations of me?

7. What am I willing to do to bring my expectations into reality?

8. How much of what I expect is within my control?

9. What is out of my control?

10. Do my expectations reflect individual interests and goals or a larger purpose?

NOTES

7 Lawrence Andrea, "Milwaukee was among first to declare racism a public health crisis," Politifact, June 18, 2020, https://www.politifact.com/factchecks/2020/jun/18/jeanette-kowalik/milwaukee-was-among-first-declare-racism-public-he/

Chapter 7

Maintaining Your Identity

P erhaps you are familiar with the old saying, "We all look alike." There have been times when I felt like I was invisible. I was "the Black one" there to make sure there was a nod to diversity, but not seen as a whole person or for who I really am. Rarely have I heard a white person questioned about their education and professional accomplishments during simple business interactions. Yet, well into my 40s and 50s, I found myself being asked to run through my CV—at the start of a conversation—to satisfy curiosity and reservations about my credentials and capabilities. While a white person's credentials and experience are assumed (even when nonexistent), we seem to start at a deficit, having to provide proof that we have what it takes. "Where did you go to school?" "How do you know __?" "How long have you __?" People will ask a litany of code questions, your answers to which will inform their judgments about you and how they choose to interact with you. What can result from these conversations is everything from positive acceptance (I didn't know Black people could do all those things), to negative resentment (Impressive, but I can't allow him/her to overshadow me!) on the part of members of the dominant group. That's right, even when everything is on par, we are somehow "graded" on a curve to keep the desired power structure intact. Remember the person who told Samantha she had no future in the organization? It turns out that person had a high school diploma and no college degree. It is not unreasonable to surmise that Samantha's education and accomplishments may have been viewed as a threat. Samantha later realized that she had recourse beyond accepting the hiring manager's negative feedback, but the impact of being told there was no future for her in the organization was profound. It took some time for her to emerge from the pall that had been cast. In the absence of a mentor or trusted advisor, she accepted the comment as truth, deferring her advancement to a position that would ultimately prove to be a win for her and the organization.

THE LONELY ONLY

As a child, I remember how excited all of us would be when seeing a Black person on television. It would usually be on the *Ed Sullivan Show* Sunday evenings, and whoever learned about it first would alert the rest of the family. I've thought of that often through the years when I've had a welcomed and unexpected encounter with another person of color. So often, we find ourselves standing alone. There isn't anyone who can relate to how we are feeling or what we are experiencing, because our reality is so different from that of our white colleagues. Added to our challenge is the necessity to practice code-switching, a term used to describe the adjustments one makes to make others feel comfortable and to gain acceptance. Like chameleons, we work to develop the desired characteristics and habits to appear to be more like others and make our perceived differences less conspicuous. But with increased comfort comes greater complexity. Once you are accepted as "one of the group," you are at risk of seeing, hearing, and experiencing things that can reveal painful and ugly truths. Suddenly you are seen as being different from other people of color, as though it is an honor or privilege to be considered "not like the others." I once heard someone refer to a young Black man as the "whitest Black person he knew," as if it was a compliment or the person had attained heightened standing in his eyes. Being an "only" can place you in very compromising positions, especially when conversations surface about colleagues of color that affirm the existence of biases and myths, the impact they have on workplace dynamics, and limitations they place on the careers of talented people who just want to do good work and be recognized for the value they bring. What also comes to light are all the things we need to consider when thinking about a game plan for career advancement.

In Chapter 4, I talked about the work we need to do outside of work. As important as this is to pay attention to, it can also be a slippery slope. At times we are faced with having to make difficult choices, especially when events and interactions involve the inclusion of family members and significant others. Now the comparisons are no longer one-to-one, but potentially family-to-family, and may involve different cultural norms, habits, and practices which become the subject of additional scrutiny. "What does your partner do?" "Where did your partner go to school?" In addition to workplace pressure, this adds a level of invasive complexity and pressure that can impact the safe place of personal relationships. We have nowhere to run, nowhere to hide …

As the saying goes, be careful what you ask for, because you might get it. Black professionals buy into code-switching and work toward greater assimilation to level the playing field and access the same opportunities as colleagues in the dominant group. With this comes assumptions that you have similar preferences and interests. Although you may have some discretion regarding unofficial out-of-office activities, official company-sponsored events are not without challenges. I've attended more than my share of executive and management retreats, in many cases at venues off the beaten path, located in places I had no personal interest in visiting, and would not have felt safe visiting alone. These outings have typically had a recreational or educational component, in some cases inappropriate for a diverse audience. In the most benign cases, it may have been a matter of different tastes in music. More serious was an incident that magnified the difference between my colleagues and me.

Story VIII

A Message from One of America's Founding Fathers

As a senior executive of a midsize firm, I was required to attend an annual senior leadership retreat. The retreat venue would change from year to year and would typically last for two to three days. Our CEO took great pride in planning the event, in some cases treating it like a family vacation. He was a self-proclaimed history buff, and he enjoyed visiting places of historical significance and was particularly fond of reenactments of actual events from years past.

One year he decided that we should visit Richmond, Virginia. Among the activities planned were a tour of antebellum architecture and a visit to St. John's Church for a reenactment of the 1775 Second Virginia Convention where Patrick Henry was said to have influenced delegates: "Give me liberty or give me death!" Once the full retreat agenda was revealed, I informed the CEO, who we will call Mike, of my discomfort with the planned events. I also let him know what I would and would not attend outside of scheduled business meetings. His response was beyond arrogant and insensitive. He was surprised by my concerns about what was just "historical content." I informed him that as a Black person, I knew more about the subject of "history" than I wanted to know, and that I was not comfortable participating in, nor did I want to discuss topics associated with the outings planned with my professional colleagues. I did my best to protect myself and my feelings.

The second night of the retreat, our group was transported by bus to Hanover Tavern for dinner. Hanover Tavern was at the core of events that took place during the American Revolution. Before dinner, several of my colleagues inquired about why I was absent from many of the planned events earlier that day, and I explained that I took advantage of being in the area and decided to spend time with a childhood friend. As dessert was being served, we were paid a visit by an actor in character as George Washington. George began to recount the events of the Second Convention. He went on to talk about all that was at stake, stating that "we had no choice but to go to war! We would have otherwise been relegated to slavery just like those Blacks."

I felt like I had been sucker-punched. Surrounded by about thirty colleagues I had known and worked with for years, at that moment I stood alone. Whatever sense of belonging I may have experienced up to that point was washed away with George's words. I immediately left the dining room and sat in the foyer until the end of the evening. Not one other person left the room, not even a white colleague who was married to a Black woman and had Black daughters. Because we had been transported by bus, I had no way of leaving the premises. Upon arrival back at our hotel, I let my manager and the HR officer know of my feelings, and that I would be leaving the retreat to return home. Let me be clear, regardless of what it may say on my business card, the sign outside my office door, or whoever you think I am: I am a Black woman first. I am unapologetic about my heritage, background, and experiences. The atrocities that have and continue to impact our right to life, liberty, and the pursuit of happiness afforded to our white counterparts are offensive to me.

I stayed at home for about two weeks trying to decide how I could and should move forward. I was enjoying my work, my involvement with high visibility projects, and learning a lot. Was this the price I would have to pay to play at this level? I also realized the incident was due more to arrogance and insensitivity and was not a malicious or intentional act. But the experience did reveal the potential pitfalls of assimilation. The sameness between me and my peers—that was assumed—exposed me to situations I could not anticipate or manage. I NEVER wanted to feel what I was feeling ever again. For me, this took being resilient to a new level. I could not help but reflect on the experiences of my great-grandfather, George Brown, during the Civil War. At the start of the war, he was a body servant for a Confederate soldier in Culpeper, Virginia. He would later be sold at a slave auction in 1862. In 1863 he seized an opportunity to escape and join Yankee troops, enabling him to enlist in a United States heavy artillery unit, where he served until 1866 and was honorably discharged. When I think about the courage, resilience, and tenaciousness that enabled him to navigate his circumstances, it inspires me to dig a little deeper and find my way to a solution.

Chapter 8

In Search of Safe Places

M any people align issues associated with workplace discrimination with corporate and business settings. In search of an environment perceived to be less competitive and more accepting of diversity, some will pursue careers in other sectors—academia, and institutions of higher learning, for example. Others may opt for business ownership and self-employment. The reality is that racism is pervasive, and the presence of people committed to discrimination is ubiquitous.

The idea that decisions informed by racism do not exist in institutions of higher learning is nothing short of a myth. Following are two stories reflecting the experiences of Maureen Hall, a career higher education professional with more than thirty years of experience. Over the course of her career, Maureen has worked in student affairs, operations, and program management, in the position of director, executive director, and assistant dean at several prestigious private and public institutions.

Story IX

Withdraw Your Application, Your Colleague Is a Better Choice

H igher education is not exempt from discrimination. I believe people think that biases do not exist in an environment composed of well-educated people whose lifework is to educate others. The reality is that people carry biases they learned as children wherever they go. Education does not necessarily remove what has been learned through life experiences. These biases are reflected in the admissions process, hiring practices, promotion, and supervision. I saw examples of discrimination in many of these functional areas. I've seen supervisors discredit or diminish an individual's performance based on skin color. The talents across a diverse group of employees are not appreciated equally. Sometimes, appearances come into play. Do these people look like me? Do they have the same level of education? Supervisors influence the culture of the organization, thereby infusing their biases throughout operations and processes. As a Black woman who worked in higher education for more than thirty years, I had many firsthand experiences with discrimination informed by the biases of both supervisors and colleagues.

On one occasion, I applied for a newly created student affairs position. It would have been a significant promotion for me, but one I had been preparing for throughout my career. One morning, a senior colleague I had worked with for more than nine years asked to meet with me. She wanted to meet to tell me that I should withdraw my application for the new role because another colleague who also applied had an advanced degree and would be a better candidate for the position. That colleague had much less experience in higher education than I had and had not been involved in student affairs. I told the colleague that we would agree to disagree.

The selection committee interviewed both the other colleague and me, and I was selected for the position. Following many notable successes, including 100 percent growth of a program, both the senior colleague and the woman she thought was a better candidate left the institution. I continued to perform successfully in the position for several years.

Story X

The Dean Thinks You Should Leave; He Feels You Are Burned Out

A new dean was hired, who was partial to people who looked like him. He created a very divisive culture and a leadership *structure that was devoid of people of color. Based on the things he would say, it appeared that he did not like people from other countries, people of color, and anyone overweight.*

In the first six months of his tenure, the dean sought reasons to discredit employees and find ways and reasons to push staff out to make room for people who fit his ideal profile. Many staff members applied for positions outside the university to get away from the toxic environment.

The dean held career discussions with several administrators. He and I talked about my career and accomplishments at the school and other positions I might be interested in. I later found out that I was on the list of people he didn't want on his staff. His operations director set up a meeting with me to advance the discussion about my identifying another position. When we met, she told me that the dean thought I was burned out and should leave. I had been in the position for more than six years and had been the recipient of the staff/faculty award of the year from the student body. I had consistently achieved the "exceeds expectations" rating in annual evaluations and was recognized as part of a group of people who helped enhance the program's reputation. Following that discussion, I asked for a meeting with the dean to discuss my conversation with his operations director. During our meeting, he told me he would be willing to provide a year of severance pay while I looked for a new position. I followed up with an email asking who my attorney should speak with to complete the severance packet agreement. The dean's office backed down on their attempt to push me out. Instead, they gave me a bad evaluation and moved me to another position within the school.

The achievement of business ownership and self-employment is an accomplishment to be celebrated. But for a person of color, it comes with its own unique challenges. Beyond the explicit barriers of securing financing and, in some cases, overcoming questions about competency, minority business owners can provoke a very menacing type of racism among members of the dominant group manifested in micro-aggressions and blatant disrespect. Following is the perspective of an experienced business owner in retail who we will identify as May.

Story XI

You Are Not Entitled to Be Here

R etail. *The word elicits a knowing eye roll, a shared grimace. Among Black women, there are thousands of stories of intended slight, purposeful delays in service, outright hostility, and bad attitudes. For Black men, it is being followed by store security and told to leave the premises. The list of egregious behavior by store and restaurant personnel is shocking in its variety, yet singular in the underlying message: you are not entitled to be here, to enjoy here. Being served is nothing to which you are entitled.*

As an artist with a retail gallery where I create and sell my art, my experience of how patrons and employees alike find inge-

nious ways to undermine, slight, and diminish the enormity of my accomplishments is vast. As I am older now, this behavior rarely provokes an angry response.

There is no deeper reflection than categorization of the offending person into a massive field of reference. As much as their intended or non-intended words or actions desire to put me into a state of non-personhood, the reverse is what prevails. They become no one to me. It is the muscle of self-preservation, self-support, and self-assertion that I have developed over the years in response to the never-ending daily assault of racist behavior. I have no idea how other Black people have managed it, but I believe we all carry the muscle memory of surviving the emotional abuse of it all. And I think it takes a toll, but being optimistic, I also believe we who are the descendants of slaves have a level of strength built into our DNA beyond any measure of what one would consider normal.

Developing the capacity to define, categorize, and protect oneself from the worst of racist behavior is a necessary skill set, and admitting to the need for it in the first place is a vital step toward empowerment and enlightenment. You deserve excellent service, you deserve your enjoyment, and you are entitled to feel safe, secure, unthreatened, and vital in whatever role your work life takes. We will never change another's behavior, and we will always have our own choices to make in our reactions to it. Choose wisely.

Choose wisely. We are consistently faced with the challenge of making difficult choices. Do we soldier on with our heads down, following a regimen of deep breathing to get through difficult situations, or do we take a stand, at times placing at risk opportunities to engage in lucrative business opportunities? Even self-employed business owners can face challenging circumstances that require us to make tough choices. I recently had to make such a choice when approached by a colleague about partnering on a potential engagement.

Story XII

I Think You're the Best Person to Facilitate a Discussion on Diversity

A colleague in my professional space appears to be interested in, but clearly struggles with how to effectively interact with Black people. Over the years, I've noticed her need to point out other people she interacts with who are Black. On occasion, she has approached me to inquire about my interest in being included as part of a coaching group that needs greater diversity. I cautioned her about this dynamic, pointing out to her that most of my clients "do not look like me," and that I hoped a need for diversity was not the only reason she thought of me in connection with professional opportunities.

This person, who I will call Mary, reached out to me about yet another engagement that included a focus on diversity. Attempting to assemble a team of three, she informed me that "given her love of teaching, she would deliver group presentations on accountability, decision-making, and other topics, so all employees are using a common language," all the things that I, too, am credentialed to discuss, and regularly address with clients. She went on to say, "I think you're the best person to facilitate a discussion on diversity," to which I replied—I'll pass.

As educated and credentialed as Mary is, she is challenged when it comes to understanding how egregiously offensive and condescending this is. Being a Black person does not, by default, make me the best person to facilitate a discussion on diversity. I am not qualified to evaluate or diagnose the psychosis that informs the biases of the white, entitled, and privileged, nor am I interested in "teaching" self-proclaimed intellectuals how to get along with Black people.

The fact that someone would address this in such a cavalier and simplistic manner suggests to me that they don't even recognize diversity, equity, and inclusion as an area that warrants training and credentialed expertise. Do they even take it seriously? I am very grateful to be in a position to say, "No thank you," and in some cases, "Hell no!" As liberating as this can be, it is not lost on me that this is not everyone's reality. Had this happened at a different time in my life or under different fiscal circumstances, it might not have been in my best interests financially to decline. In situations like this, we must find a way to draw the line. Speak up, call it out.

Chapter 9

Speaking Up, Calling Things Out

P eople who identify as being members of a minoritized group are sometimes accused of playing the race card to achieve gain in disputes that are said not to involve race. While I do not advocate meritless arguments of any kind, it has, unfortunately, become challenging to identify situations that have not been influenced at some level by skin color. Because of the stigma associated with addressing workplace inequity and bias, many people impacted will choose to let things go. I am saddened by the number of people of all ages and at all career stages who experience both subtle and overt acts of discrimination but are afraid to call it out. For fear of retribution, they soldier on in business-as-usual mode to avoid making waves—all the while dealing with the residual effects that often manifest in the form of chronic stress and poor physical and emotional health referenced earlier.

It is not easy to draw a line in the sand, but each time we let something go, we send a message of acquiescence and acceptance. In more than ten years as an executive coach, I've heard and continue to hear accounts of discrimination and circumstances that are outrageous symptoms of systemic racism, characterized by behavior that members of the dominant group would not tolerate. Few opportunities are missed to diminish notable professional accomplishments and contributions made by a member of a minority group, in some cases to be repurposed with attribution redirected to members of the dominant group.

During my first meeting with a Black female client a few years back, I asked her to describe what she wanted to achieve during our coaching engagement. Sitting at the director level in her organization, she and her team had high client visibility and were responsible for generating a significant portion of the organization's annual revenue. In an effort to provide context for goals she was setting for herself, she proceeded to recount specific experiences that primarily involved her boss, but also included interactions with colleagues. Following each discrete description, she would say, "and that's fine," chalking up what she was describing to a perceived blind spot or deficiency on her part. After about the third round, I stopped her and said, "None of this is fine!" I held up a hand-doodled sign to emphasize my point. She wept.

People believe that things will improve if they work harder, earn more certifications, put in longer hours, or volunteer to take on added responsibility. Worse is the belief that we begin to internalize that we are broken, did something wrong, or don't measure up. STOP! I've had and continue to have the privilege of working with countless talented professionals of all ages across various disciplines who believe there is something they can do to level the playing field and be treated equitably. While anything is possible, it is not likely. The degree of inherent bias embedded in many organizations' policies, practices, and systems yields to the people in power. While the most well-meaning of managers in the dominant group may recognize and, in some cases, make subtle acknowledgments of inequitable circumstances, few will be able to exercise the degree of allyship that is necessary to effect meaningful change.

Allyship can be defined as efforts made by members of a dominant group to demonstrate support of and solidarity with people who are targets of discrimination. In this era of "being woke," some of us have experienced overtures from members of the dominant group—acknowledging the existence of bias and discrimination. "You should be making more money," or "I wish I could do more, but …" While these true confessions might serve to make the person making the acknowledgment feel better, they provide little solace for a person who has persistently and consistently been the target of inequitable treatment, discrimination, and bias.

At issue are the hearts and minds of human beings. Whether discrimination is levied by an individual or is inherent in an organization's culture, it reflects values and beliefs espoused by a person or group of people in power. When thinking about addressing an occurrence or incident perceived to be out of line, it is important first to understand the source or origin. In the case of the female director, Samantha, her experience seemed to reflect her manager's blind spots that may not necessarily have been aligned with the organization's values. It would have been worthwhile for her to begin using communication tools to "unpack" situations with her manager as they occurred, and at some point, even anticipate them to take preventive measures. This would have helped her decipher what was driving her manager's behavior. Once the dynamics of a relationship have been established, it becomes more difficult to change course.

There are times when the "source" of discriminatory treatment originates outside of the relationship between manager and direct report, where the manager becomes the messenger. It is not uncommon for people to form opinions about who we are without getting to know us and for no fault of our own. People feel more comfortable with others who are like them. In the absence of familiarity, we are seen as an unknown, untested entity, placing us at an immediate disadvantage with anyone who is biased against or with unresolved feelings about people unlike themselves. It is important for us to control our own narrative telling the story of who we are and what we bring by finding ways to build relationships with key actors in an organization or context. Every person of color needs to explore two critical questions as soon as possible: (1) Who are the decision-makers in power? (2) What are their leanings regarding race, diversity, equity, and inclusion?

SUFFERING IN SILENCE

I've been saddened to hear the stories of confident, otherwise outspoken Black women who have chosen to be quiet when facing issues associated with race. For fear of placing employment at risk or not being supported, they have borne the brunt of actions, comments, circumstances, and decisions that have accommodated others at their expense. Following the humiliation of the experience itself are the lingering feelings of not having addressed the issue. "What I should have said ..." "I wanted to ..." "If I didn't need this job, I would have ..." Over time, the accumulation of these experiences renders us in a position of obedience, suppressing our voices in ways that do not serve us. For those of us who can, and in select circumstances at work and elsewhere, we have to speak up!

Developing a habit or being good at anything requires practice. When thinking about circumstances involving discrimination, inequality, equity, and exclusion, it is important to think holistically about things that make us uncomfortable in and out of the workplace that we've been willing to normalize. When have you received inferior service? When has a member of the medical profession displayed a cavalier attitude regarding your condition or concerns expressed about your health? Much like we have to breathe, we have to be willing to practice self-advocacy at all times.

ON BEING CRUSTY

This story is in memory of my beloved friend and soror, Barbara Hampton-Barclay, whose passing coincided with my work on this book. As part of our weekly Saturday morning walks, we solved the world's problems over avocado toast and coffee at our local Barnes & Noble. I often referred to Barbara as humanitarian in chief. She wanted nothing more out of this world than for everyone to be seen as humans, cared for with humanity, and have a level playing field for basic needs. She felt that using the descriptors of Black and white was divisive. As part of her quest to lessen the perceived differences among people of different ethnicities and backgrounds, she often reminded us that no one is purely Black or purely white, and that our respective complexions land on a continuum of browns, from light to dark. Rest in peace, my dear friend …

While I was a passenger on a commuter bus in June 2019, the white female bus driver and a white female passenger began a conversation about recent vacations. The driver started sharing details about her recent visit to a former plantation in Tennessee. She talked about visiting the plantation owner's house and proceeded to talk about visiting the former slave quarters. As politely as I could, I interrupted the conversation by saying, "Excuse me—I will not sit on this bus that I've paid to ride and listen to a conversation about slaves and slave quarters. Please talk about something else." The driver replied, "I am just telling her about my vacation," to which I replied, "Then invite her to have coffee or schedule a call, but that conversation cannot take place here." After a few additional insensitive exchanges, the women changed the subject.

When I shared the incident with Barbara, she grimaced, then stated, "You've gotten to be awfully crusty in your old age." I took that as a compliment and said, "Thank you, but I've been crusty my whole life." I was stunned to receive this reaction from my outspoken friend. When I asked her what she would have done, she said, "It would have made me uncomfortable, but I would not have said anything." What was of greater concern was her facial expression of raw pain and the sound of fear in her voice. As we continued to unpack our respective points of view, she shared stories of how much she had learned to tolerate over the years, feeling she had to hold back to avoid reprisal and not make others uncomfortable, especially in the workplace. Over time, the culmination of her experiences when it came to matters of race had silenced her.

I continue to have clients of color who impart stories of pain, sadness, and in some cases, borderline trauma resulting from experiences they feel powerless to address. To be quiet is the same as saying it's okay. We have to speak up!

THE MANTLE OF SPONSORSHIP

I recall being part of promotion and professional development discussions as the sole Black female executive "in the room." On one occasion, an issue on the table involved a Black female manager who had been in an "acting" role for an extended period without commensurate remuneration. She was doing a great job, in many ways raising the bar for what would be the standards and expectations for the position based on what she was able to accomplish. As we discussed whether her placement should be made permanent, and when addressing her compensation, a white male member of the senior leadership team asked, "Does she even have a degree?" Although she had been doing exceptional work, he appeared to be looking for reasons not to award her the promotion rather than trying to make it work. Thankfully, I was in the room, able to speak on her behalf. But when there is no sponsor, no ally, or anyone to speak up, decisions that don't favor us can be made for all the wrong reasons, many of which have nothing to do with our work. I watched that same colleague move mountains to recruit and hire a white female and a white male into highly visible positions based on his perceptions—no data—of who they were and what they could do. Compensated at the highest levels, both had short tenures, leaving behind significant collateral damage due to their lack of competence and work ethic. The inclinations and actions of this decision-maker provided a good example of the significance of familiarity. When faced with a human capital decision involving a person unlike himself whom he did not know, his default was skepticism. Even without the benefit of relevant information, he felt more comfortable taking a chance on people who looked like him and whom he perceived to be more like himself.

Getting to know people throughout the organization and allowing them to get to know you is important. We may have different interests, and in many cases, we won't like the same things. But not breaking the barrier of unfamiliarity can place us at a significant disadvantage as minorities. An important aspect of onboarding at a new company or in a new role is determining who you need to know and who you want to know. The effort to build rapport should precede needs that may arise to address a sensitive issue or have a difficult conversation. Establishing relationships helps us to be seen as less the anomaly and perhaps more like everyone else than expected. In some cases, it may help to remove or at least minimize some of the limiting obstacles and barriers to be overcome.

While an organization's messaging about diversity is helpful, an accurate measure of commitment is reflected in what actually takes place. There are some cases where there appears to be a good mix of employees representing different races and ethnicities; at issue is what roles they play within the organization. A 2021 study conducted by McKinsey, entitled "Race in the Workplace,"[8] revealed that Black employees represented 18 percent of frontline employees, and 7 percent of managerial employees among participating respondents. When looking at executive-level jobs in the U.S. private sector, that number drops to 3 percent, and is even lower among Fortune 500 companies. The study also revealed a revolving door in entry-level jobs and a broken rung on the ladder to managerial roles, with only one in three or four reporting that they have a sponsor or the support they need to advance. This is juxtaposed with 87 percent of participating companies reporting that they have a sponsorship program in place.

Even when diversity appears to have been achieved throughout an organization, it is important to pay attention to other details, especially when it comes to compensation. I recall a situation involving a Black female executive who had full access to the company's compensation and benefits information as part of her role. While working on a project for the CEO, she discovered that her peers and colleagues at similar organizational levels were being compensated at significantly higher levels than she was being compensated. When she addressed this with the CEO, he attempted to reassure her by letting her know how important she was to the company, committing that he would "do what he could" to address the deficiency in her compensation. She left the company and has moved on.

There seems to be a sentiment among many that we should be grateful for what we are given. We should be happy to be earning a high salary, even when it is not on par with what our counterparts in similar and in some cases lesser positions are earning. When it becomes a veil for complacency, gratitude can be a hindrance to the very things we want to achieve. Merriam-Webster defines complacency as self-satisfaction, especially when accompanied by unawareness of actual dangers or deficiencies. So, as we express gratitude, for example, for earning a

$150,000 salary, we find complacency in the fact that it allows us to live comfortably, and it is perhaps the highest salary we've ever received. We lose sight of the possibility that our $150,000 is only 75% of what our counterparts are earning in the same position.

At the core of inequality are issues grounded in economics, from requirements for basic subsistence to the accumulation of wealth. A 2021 study conducted by McKinsey & Company revealed that the median Black household has about one-eighth of the wealth held by the median white household. In actual dollar amounts, this is the difference between $24,000 and $188,000. Only 2 percent of Black families have a net worth above $1 million, compared to 16 percent of white families.[9] The idea that we should be grateful for what we earn, regardless of how closely it is aligned with our value, is a condescending insult. When I hear someone celebrate earning a six-figure salary, my reaction is often—why shouldn't you be earning six figures? How much do your colleagues earn? We can't be so busy being grateful that we fail to practice stewardship over our earning power and the value we bring.

We can't be afraid to address experiences that are beyond the pale. But our challenges and responses need to be factual and well-grounded, and reflect realistic expectations based on the environment and the circumstances involved. They must especially be well thought out. We have to speak out!

WHAT IF I HAD ...

Think of a time when you experienced something that made you uncomfortable and didn't say anything:
1. What held you back?

2. What was at risk?

3. Given a replay, what would you say? What would you do?

4. How did you process and make meaning of what you experienced?

5. What would you do if the same thing happened to you again?

NOTES

8 "Race in the workplace: The Black experience in the US private sector," McKinsey & Co., February 21, 2021, https://www.mckinsey.com/featured-insights/diversity-and-inclusion/race-in-the-workplace-the-black-experience-in-the-us-private-sector

9 "The Economic State of Black America: What is and what could be," McKinsey Global Institute, June 17, 2021, https://www.mckinsey.com/featured-insights/diversity-and-inclusion/the-economic-state-of-Black-America-what-is-and-what-could-be

Access Denied

CONCLUSION

The anecdotes and stories shared span a period of more than fifty years. During that time, countless innovations have evolved to become mainstays in our lives: coronary bypass surgery (1967); the invention of the cell phone (1973); laptop computers (1981) and the Internet (1989); text messaging (1992); and the iPad (2010), to name a few. But in many ways, minoritized groups remain on a hamster wheel and continue to run in place, making relatively little progress when it comes to having a proportionate share of the prosperity we played such an active and meaningful role in creating. In much the same way a movie score sets the tone for a film, many in the majority group are committed to a schema that mitigates minoritized groups' aptitude, capabilities, intellect, and humanity. Even when new information is introduced that would suggest otherwise, it is suppressed. Holding tight to the idea that minority groups are defined solely by slavery and positions of servitude that place the majority in a position of superiority enables many to hold on to positions of power to which they believe they are entitled.

Consider the fact that it took fifty years for the world to learn about and celebrate the achievements of Katherine Johnson, a Black American mathematician whose calculations of orbital mechanics were critical to the success of the space program at NASA. And consider Paul Williams, the trailblazing Black architect who designed homes for the stars in Los Angeles, California, in neighborhoods where he could not have lived because of his race. In addition to a client list that included Frank Sinatra, Lucille Ball and Desi Arnaz, and Barbara Stanwyck, Mr. Williams also designed many public and private buildings. And when was someone going to say something about Black Wall Street in Tulsa, Oklahoma? Much like a criminal record being expunged, the massacre that obliterated one of the most prominent African American business communities in the United States during the early 20th century was shrugged off as if nothing happened. We've recently learned about Nathan "Uncle Nearest" Green, the Black man who taught Jack Daniel how to make whiskey while working at the distillery in the late 1880s. The list goes on, and there are no doubt countless truths yet to be revealed.

Based on the sixty-plus years I have been impacted by and witnessed indiscretions that have a foundation of bias and prejudice, I have no illusions that hearts and minds will be transformed, or that true allyship will take hold to the extent necessary for meaningful change to occur any time soon. And although hopeful, I know that hope is not the elixir that will be required to make a difference. Much like developing a strategic objective and plan for the companies that employ us, or for our own businesses, we must develop a strategic and intentional plan for how we will move ourselves forward that is realistic, and includes provisions for us to defend and compete for what rightfully belongs to us. Life is short, and we cannot afford to wait for someone else to decide if and when we should be granted a nod for something we have worked for, earned, deserve, and in some cases are entitled to. Of course, we cannot lose hope, but hope is not a strategy.

In the words of our contributor, May –

After years of endurance, after years of trying to understand, define, accept, minimize, and educate, I believe now the uphill path leading to the goal of shared compassion requires admission of the enormity of the wrong done. In Alcoholics Anonymous, this is called the step where one admits to being an alcoholic. Here, it is the step where the descendants of slave owners and those who look like them realize that the exalted economic and social status they lay claim to was actually forged on the backs of unwilling, captive, and traumatized people for more than 300 years.

Slavery was no hiccup of circumstance in the development of humanity. It was and still is an ingrained, systematic, deep-seated, long-enduring vein of pure indoctrination, dogma, propaganda, legal, physical, mental, and emotional abuse inflicted on people of color for the often hidden but definitively seen result of economic superiority. We want to believe racism is about skin color, and it is not. It is about money, opportunity, advancement, control, power, and nowhere are the machinations of this played out more succinctly than in the workplace.

Mental boundaries and limits will advance you only to the degree that you can work and carry out your day-to-day survival needs in a bubble, autonomously. If you are required to enter the fray of working with other associates or with the public, then you will be at the mercy of the forces that govern those intersections of culture and difference.

Maybe you saw yourself in one of the stories shared, or some of the anecdotes made you think about an experience differently. I hope you will consider opportunities that exist to enhance the stewardship of your professional life and personal circumstances. Perhaps this begins with examining the alignment between your expectations and the reality of your professional context—and the actors involved. Next might be the establishment and activation of your advisory team or peer network to help make meaning of your findings. Whatever course you choose, please don't wait for someone who is operating from the position of their best interests, not yours, to decide what you are worth and when you will be "worthy." This is not a dress rehearsal. Do what you can to live the life you want for yourself.

RESOURCES

Let's continue the conversation! If any of the stories and experiences shared resonated with you, and you are a member of the BIPOC community, you are invited to be part of an ongoing dialogue. Consider this a *safe place,* to connect with people who *look like you and can relate to your experiences.* Together, we want to explore and work through common challenges, as well as share and access resources that will help you navigate your professional space more effectively.

Please visit www.access-denied.net/letstalk to share your interest and preferences for keeping in touch, or send an email to conversations@access-denied.net.

A NOTE FROM THE AUTHOR

Thank you for choosing to add *Access Denied* to your library, and especially for taking the time to read, and hopefully absorb and process what the stories convey.

In a most unexpected way, events of recent years augmented by experiences I continue to have as a Black woman have landed on me as a call to action. Without a notable platform, it is difficult to discern how to make a meaningful impact. I thought that sharing stories that reflect a variety of disciplines, age groups, and points in time might inspire others to act, and to think about what they can do to influence changes, even if on a small scale.

As I began collecting stories, I could not have imagined that this choir of voices, each sharing their unique experiences, would have harmonized into such a resounding melody, albeit with troubling lyrics. I also had no idea of what to expect regarding the receptiveness of the publishing community and a willingness to allow the truth to be told. Though not surprised, I was disappointed by the response I received from some of the firms I approached, including some that profess to be in support of publications that address diversity, equity, and inclusion. In one case, for example, I received immediate pushback on the cover art. Without curiosity about its meaning, interest in what it represented or any conversation, here is one response I received about 45 minutes after sharing my manuscript and artwork:

Hi Brenda,

I just wanted to provide some feedback from our team on the possible cover. We would highly recommend redoing it for the retail market. The current mockup is not bad, but it's also not necessarily appropriate for the genre or the topic, and one of the first impressions was that it looked like a children's book cover before they were able to read the subtitle. Packaging will be one of the most important aspects of any book, and our teams will work together, and with you as well, to come up with appropriate options for the retail market.

As this message reflects, we continue to be invisible in the eyes of many, with no regard for who we are. I respectfully directed the company to delete my file and moved on.

Beyond the call to action, I've felt a great sense of urgency to connect and share. Rather than continuing to waste time trying to identify a firm with whom I could share creative and editorial synergy, I decided to engage the best professional guidance I could find and publish under the name of South Columbus Avenue Press, named for the street where I grew up, where my earliest impressions of life were formed. A very special thank you to our dear friend Frank Austin for helping me to reminisce about life on S. Columbus Ave. near E. Third St. in the logo he created.

ABOUT THE AUTHOR

Brenda Harrington, PCC, is a Certified Executive Coach and leadership development facilitator. The founder of Adaptive Leadership Strategies LLC, she works with leaders globally in public, private, government, intergovernmental, humanitarian, and nonprofit organizations. Through one-on-one executive coaching, team coaching, group facilitation and interventions, she focuses on helping clients embrace, nurture, and develop their innate and unique attributes so that they can manifest the best possible version of their professional selves.

Before establishing Adaptive Leadership Strategies, Brenda spent more than thirty years in private industry. Having held positions ranging from first-level management to senior executive leadership, she has had countless first-hand experiences with issues involving diversity, both explicit and implied. In her coaching practice, some of the circumstances she encounters with clients and within organizations involving diversity, inclusion and acceptance mirror experiences she has had, or has been aware of over many years. Her concern and the *why* inspiring her to assemble this collection of stories is to enhance awareness and preparedness for those who are impacted by a lack of diversity and resistance to acceptance and inclusion. She knows that in the absence of mentors, sponsors, and people who have our best interests at heart, professional obstacles are more formidable. When all you hear is that you can't or that you shouldn't, chances are that you don't and you won't. Brenda believes that in many cases *can't* means that you *can*, and that *shouldn't* often means yes—you *should!*

Brenda is a graduate of the Georgetown University Leadership Coaching program and is a credentialed member of the International Coaching Federation. She holds a master's degree from Virginia Polytechnic Institute and State University, Pamplin College of Business, and a bachelor's degree from Adelphi University. Brenda is certified to administer several psychometric assessments. In addition to leadership development facilitation, she also facilitates programs on emotional intelligence and global mindset.

ABOUT THE ILLUSTRATOR

Dr. Jeanette Kowalik comes from a long line of creatives. As a child, she discovered her talent for the visual arts from a dream. She also attended art schools from first to eighth grade in her hometown of Milwaukee, Wisconsin. Jeanette was determined to have a career in the arts but faced two major obstacles along the way. One was racism and the other was financial. In middle school, a teacher questioned Jeanette's goal of becoming a fashion designer because they claimed "Africans don't wear clothes." This discouraged Jeanette more than she realized. As for the financial barrier, Jeanette was unable to afford tuition at the Milwaukee Institute of Art and Design. A career in the arts was out of reach for Jeanette, or so she thought.

After high school graduation, Dr. Kowalik attended the University of Wisconsin-Milwaukee (UWM), where she found her career in public health. During her time at UWM, she had to pivot to raising her son, working, and completing her studies to rise out of poverty. These circumstances, like those of many other teen parents in similar environments, diverted Jeanette's time away from creating art because she had to make money. Over the years, Jeanette developed pieces whenever she could, mainly using acrylic or oil paints. Jeanette found solace and joy in crossing pop and hip-hop culture by Black folk and Ancient Egyptian art—her first love of style and form.

"I am elated that Brenda asked me to develop the cover art for this motivational and moving work. She has reactivated a creative spark in me that has realigned me with my original call to service—to translate messages from divine soul and ancestral spirits, human emotion, and the signs of the times into beautiful and provocative works of art. I am forever thankful!"

Today, Dr. Kowalik is the President and Owner of Jael Solutions Consulting Services, LLC. With 20 years of dynamic public health experience, she supports organizations and communities through bold, equity-centered consulting on matters involving public health. For more information, please visit www.jaelPhD.com

Access Denied

Made in the USA
Middletown, DE
04 September 2024

60105674R00084